How to PLAN YOUR LIFE

HOW TO PLAN YOUR LIFE

Revised and Enlarged Edition

JIM DAVIDSON

A FIREBIRD PRESS BOOK

PELICAN PUBLISHING COMPANY
Gretna 1998

Copyright © 1979, 1986
By Jim Davidson
All rights reserved

Library of Congress Cataloging-in-Publication Data

Davidson, Jim.
    How to plan your life.

    1. Conduct of life. I. Title.
BJ1581.2.D367 1986   158'.1   86-2476
ISBN 1-56554-498-6

Manufactured in the United States of America
Published by Pelican Publishing Company, Inc.
1000 Burmaster Street, Gretna, Louisiana 70053

*This book is affectionately dedicated to
my good friend J. D. Barnett, Jr.,
to honor his exemplary life,
his commitment to excellence,
his years of faithful service,
and his enormous contribution to his country.*

Contents

Preface 11
Acknowledgments 15
The "How to PLAN YOUR LIFE" Master Concept 19
A Glossary of Important Terms
    in Layman's Language 23

Part One   **Who Am I?** 35
    Chapter 1   A New Beginning 37
    Chapter 2   Self-Image: How It Controls Your Life 43
    Chapter 3   Why Goals Are Important for You 51

Part Two   **Where Am I?** 55
    Chapter 4   Time for a Check-Up: Your Personal Inventory 57
    Chapter 5   The Human Mind and How It Functions 63
    Chapter 6   Your Greatest Power: The Power to Choose 69

8 How to PLAN YOUR LIFE

 Chapter 7 Good Health: The Key to Long-Lasting Success 77

Part Three **Where Am I Going in Life?** 85
 Chapter 8 The Prelude to Success: What Success Means to You 87
 Chapter 9 Achieving Success by Meeting the Needs of Others 93
 Chapter 10 Goals: How to Set Them and Reach Them 99
 Chapter 11 Can Goals Be Too Big? 107

Part Four **How Will I Get There?** 113
 Chapter 12 A Career or a Job? 115
 Chapter 13 Natural Laws and How They Affect Our Lives 121
 Chapter 14 The Demands of True and Long-Lasting Success 133

Part Five **What Kind of Person Will I Be?** 139
 Chapter 15 Self-Examination: Values, Priorities, and Rewards 141
 Chapter 16 Spiritual Life: An Often Untapped Power 149
 Chapter 17 The Role of the Traditional American Family 155
 Chapter 18 The American Free Enterprise System 161
 Chapter 19 Income for Present Need and Future Security 169

Part Six		What Must I Do to Make Success Happen? 179
Chapter 20		Managing and Using Time 181
Chapter 21		The Force of Personal Habits 189
Chapter 22		Good Communication Skills 195
Chapter 23		The Life-Long Process of Continuing Education 203

America—The Place for Success 211
A Personal Note from the Author 219
For Your Information 221

Most people spend more time planning a party or a vacation than they do in planning their lives. Do you agree?

Preface

One evening back in May, 1973, I was the commencement speaker for a small high school in my home state of Arkansas. Following my commencement address that evening, I saw eighty high school seniors awarded their diplomas. As I sat there, I was struck by a thought that was to completely change my life. I will tell you about that thought in a moment, but for you to have some understanding of why it was so life changing, please allow me to share this background information with you.

Prior to that fateful night in 1973, I had been involved in a number of different jobs and careers, ranging from driving a laundry truck to working in a parts warehouse, from production work in a printing company to a later position as an outside printing salesman. During my sales career I felt the need to take a public speaking course. Shortly thereafter, my speech instructor suggested that we form a company to distribute motivation programs being produced on cassette tapes.

It was not long until this idea became a reality. I began to talk with prospects about the benefits of a motivation program. As time went by, I had many people say to me, "Jim, why don't you work with our school teachers to motivate students to see the value of a good education, before they get our of school and it's too late?" As a result, it became apparent to me that the real need for this kind of information was in our nation's schools and colleges.

I began to call on decision makers in our schools, most of whom greeted me with open arms. They not only purchased motivation programs, they invited me to provide in-service training for their teachers and to speak to students in a variety of settings: assembly programs, banquets, career days, and commencement exercises.

Working with students over the years as a businessman, I have learned from first-hand experience that most students have no goals other than going to school and receiving a diploma. Beyond this meager aim, they have no idea what they want to do with their lives.

If this discovery was not enough to motivate me to do something, I had also learned that changing technology had produced thousands of new jobs and careers, and that society had become much more complex than it was in the days of our forefathers. In the early years of our nation's history, high schools were structured as "prep schools" to prepare students to go on to college. For those who did not continue higher education there were a limited number of options, such as farming, business, or the military. But advanced technology and the migration of people from rural to urban areas of our country have drastically changed this. Today, about seventy percent of all jobs in society require some type of vocational or technical skill.

Regardless of what their opportunities were, I knew from first-hand experience that shortly after graduation many of these students would be on the streets looking for jobs. I also knew, because I had been down that same road a few years before myself, that when they married and had families to support and regular bills to pay, it would not be long before they would feel trapped. With inflation eating away at an income already low because of a lack of education or skill training, this situation would produce failures and cynics detrimental to our country, and it would be tragic for the individuals themselves.

When a young person nears graduation, he or she faces a multitude of choices in planning his or her life and career. Formal education should have provided basic skills, subject matter, and a limited degree of insight into the world of work. In most cases, however, our nation's educational system does not teach students how to set and reach goals, how to develop a positive mental attitude, how to foster a healthy self-image, how to achieve financial security, and how the competitive American free enterprise system works and what must be done if we are to preserve it.

Without receiving this kind of training during their formal schooling, I don't think it is too likely that people will somehow find it on their own later in life. As a result, we see millions of people today who have no real purpose in life, no written, clear-cut goals, and no plans for the future. In a land where a banquet is prepared every day, most people are settling for a sandwich.

My original observations back in 1973 inspired me to write and publish a booklet titled *Jim Davidson's Life Plan*. I must confess that twelve years' experience in the printing business played some part in my decision, but twenty thousand copies were printed and sold to individuals, business firms, schools, and colleges. Later, many of these same ideas were incorporated in the first edition of *How To PLAN YOUR LIFE*. In 1979 I began a daily radio program with the same name, which can now be heard on many radio stations. The research necessary to write and record over one thousand three-minute radio shows has produced a tremendous number of new ideas, poems, and quotations. Many of these have been incorporated into this revised edition. My hope and prayer is that you will read this book and enjoy and benefit immensely from it.

Acknowledgments

Since no person achieves success without the help and encouragement of others, I would be remiss if I did not acknowledge my debt and express my heartfelt appreciation to some very special people. These people are very special to me because they have helped me, encouraged me, and believed in me over the years.

Unfortunately, space will not permit me to list all the individuals I would like to include personally, so I simply say to all of you whose names do not appear here: if you have helped, inspired or be-friended me, you know who you are—Thank you!

Heading my list is my wonderful wife, Viola. Her beauty, charm, and sweet spirit make life worth living and keep a spring in my gait. Her love, devotion, and encouragement over the years I have deeply appreciated.

My mother, Mrs. Montine McDonnell, is and always has been by my side to help. I know I can count on her love even when I do not deserve it.

My father, W. A. Davidson, is gone now, but he did a job on me while he was here. He did his best to teach me right from wrong.

Mrs. Martha Hawley, a special fourth grade teacher, whipped me when I needed to be whipped and loved me when I needed to be loved.

Dr. W. C. Hobgood, my favorite college professor, was special to many people, but somehow I got the feeling he cared for me in a personal way.

Bert Parke, president of Democrat Printing and Lithographing Company in Little Rock, Arkansas, believed in me and got me started down the road to success. (Do not ask him about it, though, because he will probably deny it.)

Bob Gannaway, my former Dale Carnegie instructor and business partner, is the greatest role model a young man could ever have.

It was my privilege to represent Earl Nightingale's motivational materials in the State of Arkansas. Through personal contacts with him and the influence of his recordings, my mind was opened to some of the secrets of the universe.

A chance meeting in 1971 in Chicago, Illinois, began my friendship with Win Pendleton. As the author of many books, he encouraged me to write my own, and was largely responsible for the first edition of this book being published.

Ed Riddick, a highly successful engineer and businessman, helped me get started in a new career. He came along to encourage and inspire me just when I needed it most.

My thanks to thousands of close friends in the field of education—State Department personnel, administrators, teachers, and students who have been a joy to serve and to know. They also provided a classroom setting for my hands-on experience.

My "How to Plan Your Life" radio program sponsors and station managers make it possible for my ideas to reach the people in their communities who also need help and encouragement in their daily lives.

Again, to all of you, thank you from the bottom of my heart!

How to PLAN YOUR LIFE

The "How to Plan Your Life" Master Concept

It is important here in the beginning to briefly discuss the overall plan or method I will be using to present the "How to PLAN YOUR LIFE" concept to you (a concept being a collection of thoughts and ideas). If you can somehow get a "feel" for my thinking and see the whole picture, the benefits will be far greater than what you would achieve just reading one chapter at a time. I'd like for you to clearly understand the essence of the "How to PLAN YOUR LIFE" master concept.

As a human resources consultant and professional speaker for over twenty years, one thing I have found to be consistently true is that, down deep, most people want to be successes in life. To be sure, I have encountered many people who were discouraged and disillusioned and did not think it was possible for them to win, but even those people really wanted to succeed.

The word "success" means different things to different people (I will discuss this in detail later), but one of my first basic questions was "What really makes a person successful?" In order to discover the real foundation of success I began to collect information, listen to tapes, do interviews, and read everything I could find on the subject. Slowly but surely, some answers began to emerge.

After several years, I reached the conclusion that there were two distinct areas to consider: the person and the career, job, or activities in which the person wants to be successful. Obviously, no one person can be a success at everything. To have some order or framework for this research, I decided to enlist the aid of six open-ended questions. Notice how they lead logically from one to another.

1. Who Am I?
2. Where Am I?
3. Where Am I Going in Life?
4. How Will I Get There?
5. What Kind of Person Will I Be?
6. What Must I Do to Make Success Happen?

When you finish reading this introduction, take a few minutes and skim through the rest of the book. Begin with Part One, Who Am I? Read the title of each chapter, and go on to Part Two, Where Am I? and repeat the process. Before you get to the end of the book, you will see how this concept begins to unfold.

My planning approach has been developed after many years of experience. I am a great believer in "motivation" and know it is a very important ingredient for success, but if you are not careful, it can be very superficial and shallow and wear off very quickly. Motivation is somewhat like taking a bath—you know how long a bath lasts, even a great one. While short- and long-term planning, on the other hand, may not be as exciting in the beginning, it will without question provide a more stable foundation for long-lasting and permanent success. And I have to believe this is what you want.

I consider it a real privilege to have the opportunity to share these ideas with you. If you will read this book, think about the ideas and concepts presented here, go back and reread it again, fill it out as a personal plan for your life, and take the appropriate action, your life will never be the same again. You will have a better self-image, a more positive mental attitude, specific, written goals, a better understanding of our economic system, a financial plan for your future, better awareness of your personal priorities in the areas of spiritual things, family, career, and income, and you will know what you must do well each day to keep living a happy, rewarding and successful life.

FOOD FOR THOUGHT:

Opportunity

They do me wrong who say I come no more
    When once I knock and fail to find you in;
For every day I stand outside your door
    And bid you wake, and rise to fight and win.

Wail not for precious chances passed away.
    Weep not for golden ages on the wane!
Each night I burn the records for the day;
    At sunrise every soul is born again.

Laugh like a boy at splendors that have sped.
    To vanished joys be blind and deaf and dumb;
My judgements seal the dead past with its dead,
    But never bind a moment yet to come.

Tho' deep in mire, wring not your hands and weep;
    I lend my arm to all who say, "I can!"
No shame-faced outcast ever sank so deep
    But yet might rise and be again a man.

Dost thou behold thy lost youth all aghast?
    Dost reel from righteous retribution's blow?
Then turn from blotted archives of the past
    And find the future's pages white as snow.

Art thou a mourner? Rouse thee from thy spell;
    Art thou a sinner? Sins may be forgiven;
Each morning gives thee wings to flee from hell,
    Each night a star to guide thy feet to Heaven.

—Walter Malone

If you ever feel like you have reached the end of your rope, tie a knot and hang on! Help is on the way.

A Glossary of Important Terms in Layman's Language

I have been privileged hundreds of times to speak to audiences in almost every area of society. In doing so, I have found that one of the most important ingredients for success was to make sure I was speaking the language of my listeners. This was true whether it was a class of fifth graders, a sales meeting for a large company, a college faculty conference, a Chamber of Commerce banquet, a convention, or a ladies' night at a civic club. Yes, to be successful communicators, we must first have something to say that is of interest, and then choose the proper words to express our thoughts and ideas so they will be clearly understood.

For this reason, I am including a series of definitions of important terms in layman's language here at the front of this book rather than in the back as is customarily done. I'd like to make sure from the start that we are speaking the same language. Depending on your age, education, vocabulary, and level of intellectual development, a quick review may be all that is necessary for you to get the maximum benefits. It is possible of course that you may want to do an extensive study of these terms to gain new insights that will enhance the concepts presented on the following pages. No systematic attempt

There is no way we can come up with it if it isn't already there. True?

has been made to re-write the dictionary or try to include all the terms that apply to the subject at hand. Ready access to the meanings of some of the important terms used in this book will make it easier to read and understand, and therefore will make it much more valuable to you. Another important consideration is that some of the following words have more than one meaning. I am only including definitions as they apply to the concepts presented here.

accomplishment: the end result of a goal, plan, or objective. "Her *accomplishment* was the fruit of careful planning and hard work."

assessment: a method devised to evaluate a person's progress; similar to a test; can also be applied to places and events. "Taking time now to do an *assessment* could save you time and money later."

accountability: a system devised to hold people responsible for their actions. "If a company does not insist on the *accountability* of its employees, the company will fail or will have serious financial problems."

attitude: the outward expression of inward thoughts and feelings. "You could tell he had a good *attitude* by the cheerful, positive way he conducted himself."

automatic: without thinking or reflection. "He did not have to think about it; his response was *automatic*."

basic needs: the needs every person has: food, shelter, clothing, transportation, and medical care. "Until we satisfy our *basic needs*, there is little or no motivation to strive for the finer things of life."

basic skills: those skills necessary to function in today's society: reading, writing, mathematics, driving a car, keeping records, domestic skills, personal hygiene, and so on. "*Basic skills* are absolutely necessary for a person to function as a responsible member of today's society."

body language: the means of expression a person has without the written or spoken word; a form of nonverbal communication. "Often a person's *body language*—gestures, eye contact, posture—speak more loudly than the spoken words."

career: the choice a person makes as a long-term means of earning a living; usually different from a job in that it requires more education, a deeper commitment, and a progressive attitude adaptable to change. "With over fifty thousand choices in our society, practically every person can have an exciting *career*, thereby earning both financial and personal rewards."

cause and effect: the natural law that controls everything in the universe: for every action there is an equal and opposite reaction; good actions equal good results, and bad actions equal bad results. "I thought I was lucky until I discovered that the law of *cause and effect* established the consequences of my efforts."

character: the outward expression of a person's total personality, including attitudes, actions, and habits; formed in early childhood, character literally controls our lives. A person with good character has a better chance for success. "What I like most about John is that he posesses excellent *character*—you can always count on him to do what is right."

commitment: a firm decision to perform or not to perform some action, involving a person's total resources in the mental, physical, moral, and spiritual areas of life. "Marriage is a *commitment* for life—without that foundation marriage will not last."

conscious mind: that portion of our minds that is alert, awake, and receives input through one or more of the the five senses: sight, hearing, taste, touch, and smell. "The longer you think about an idea by keeping it in your *conscious mind*, the clearer the idea will become."

creativity: the making or rearranging of new things from old things (a pipe from a corncob, for example); also applies to ideas that are not expressed in a traditional way. "There are many technological and artistic products available in our world because of the *creativity* of some very talented people."

democracy: a system of government wherein the majority rules. "The United States of America is a representative *democracy*."

dignity: the process of evaluation whereby people recognize their individual worth and value. "To do that menial task would be beneath his *dignity*."

enthusiasm: (from the Greek "entheos," meaning, "full of the god" or "inspired") a source of new energy we all have, just waiting to be used. "Tom's *enthusiasm* helped him get more done in a shorter period of time."

free enterprise: a unique economic system in which individuals and groups of individuals own production facilities and produce goods and services to meet consumer needs and wants; controlled by the law of supply and demand, its primary motive is profit. "The countries of the world with the highest standards of living allow their citizens to participate in *free enterprise*."

financial security: the position in society where an individual is free from the pressures and demands of meeting day to day obligations; in most cases, also involves living a higher than average lifestyle. "Most people desire to achieve *financial security* and escape the worries of limited income and the uncertainty of money needs in the future."

goal: something specific, realistic, and obtainable, that an individual or a group of individuals decide they would like to have or would like to be; should be written down on paper. "The person with no *goal* could be compared to the ship that has no rudder."

habit: an action performed without conscious thought; formed by repeating the same action over and over again. "I'd like to stop smoking but now that it's a *habit*, it rules me."

higher needs: those needs that human beings seek after satisfying the law of self-preservation, the first law of nature. "My most important *higher needs* are companionship and spiritual growth."

imagination: a unique capability of the human mind to combine subconscious information to produce mental pictures. "The child has a vivid *imagination*—just look at the pictures she has drawn."

income: what a person or organization receives from production, including money and other material things; also includes intangible or psychological rewards as well. "How much *income* per month do you really need to live comfortably and obtain satisfaction?"

intangible: not able to be seen or touched. Intangible or psychological rewards include satisfaction, pride, and accomplishment. "Even though Susan did not have a lot of material things she was happy with the *intangible* rewards she had received."

integrity: a greatly desired personal quality that is evidenced by actions that are morally right, even when the person is sure no one would ever know the difference. "The person who has *integrity* can always be counted on to do a good job at a good value."

inventory: a check-up to count, evaluate, or assess what a person or organization has; includes tangible and intangible things. "Our store is closed this week, because we are taking *inventory* of our product stock."

investment: something done with time, money, or other resources that is designed to increase the value of those resources. "*Investment* of money has the goal of earning more money—$1000 at 10 percent annual interest yields $100. This $100 could be called the fruits or rewards of the investment."

job: a task or form of employment engaged in to receive an hourly, weekly, or monthly salary, the proceeds of which go to meet basic needs; distinguished from career by different educational resources and long-term commitment. "My *job* is not really fun, but it does bring home a paycheck."

learning process: the means by which people collect and store information in their subconscious minds; can be structured, as in a course of study, or can arise from the experiences of everyday life; also includes the development and acquisition of talents and skills. "The *learning process* does not take place solely in school, but formal education is an important part of it."

money: a form of wealth; in our society, a medium of exchange—it is what we receive for our production which can then be exchanged or traded for the production of others. "Sometimes people make the mistake of marrying for *money*."

morality: compliance or noncompliance with moral law. The moral standards in the United States are basically from the Bible, as is evidenced by the fact that our country is largely a Christian nation. "You don't have to belong to a church or synagogue to adhere to basic decency and *morality.*"

natural laws: those laws or principles created by the unchanging forces of nature; examples include the law of gravity, the law of cause and effect, the law of motion, and the law of natural selection. When we learn how to work on the right side of natural laws, our chances for success become greatly increased. "There are many *natural laws* that affect our lives and actions whether or not we know about them."

nonverbal communication: all methods of transmitting words or mental images without the aid of the spoken word; examples are writing, sign language, body language, Braille, and Morse code. (*See also* verbal communication.) "Martha wasn't an exceptional speaker, but her *nonverbal communication* skills helped her get her message across to others."

opportunity: a condition created by a political and economic system whereby individuals or groups of individuals are motivated by the idea of personal gain. "Immigrants are still attracted to America because it is the 'land of *opportunity*'—possibilities for success are wide open."

persistence: a personal quality a person has or develops that includes staying power, determination, and a commitment to stick with a goal, job, or task to its logical conclusion, or until all avenues for possible success have been exhausted. "*Persistence* is the success quality of trying again whenever you don't quite succeed."

potential: that which is possible in any given area of life such as in the areas of mental, physical, and economic development. It has been determined that most people use only five to ten percent of their true mental potential. "Young people have a great deal of *potential*—their whole lives are still before them."

predetermined: set prior to action actually being taken; used to describe goals, decisions, or courses of action. "If your goals are *predetermined*, the path to success will be clearly set out before you."

priorities: a system of ranking the most significant things in life in order of their importance. "When you send a package by *priority* mail, the post office should take special care of it."

private sector: that portion of our economic system owned, maintained, and managed by private citizens; distinguished from the public sector, which is controlled by some agency of national, state, or local government. "Business in the *private sector* must earn profits in order to survive."

procrastination: delay or deferral in making a decision or choosing a course of action; the inability to act or make a decision quickly. "*Procrastination* is always an easy path, but success requires that you act immediately when the time is right."

production: the development, manufacture, and distribution of goods and services; followed by sale to consumers for a profit or to the government for distribution to needy individuals; the total amount of production of goods and services for a country in a given year is known as the Gross National Product or GNP. " In recent years *production* has increased more rapidly in Japan than it has in the United States."

profit: the difference between the total cost of production and the selling price; provides salaries, fringe benefits, return on investment, expansion capital, and a tax base for all public services; most important ingredient in the free enterprise system. "I got a raise because sales in my company were up this year and *profit* increased."

public sector: the portion of our economic system controlled by some agency of national, state, or local government that is in existence to provide services to citizens that theoretically cannot provide those services for themselves; agencies funded and maintained by taxes paid by citizens employed in both the public and private sectors. "When I went to work for the highway department I didn't think about it being a part of the *public sector.*"

purpose: a reason or mental, moral, or spiritual commitment to pursue a certain course of action. "My *purpose* is to build a successful business, and I'm going to stick to that task until it is completed."

repetition: performance of the same action over and over again; reoccurrence at regular intervals; one of the basic ways information is stored in the subconscious mind. "Learning multiplication tables by *repetition* might be boring, but it's the best way to remember them."

reward: the goal or end result of labor and efforts; the satisfaction rendered by good work, whether it is money from our employment or a gold medal for finishing first in an Olympic event. "Susan was motivated to stay with her job because she enjoyed the work and also because it offered financial and personal *rewards.*"

savings plan: a carefully considered written course of action developed by a person or group of persons to set aside or invest a portion of income for use at some future point in time. "I developed a *savings plan* when I was nineteen, and I now enjoy the benefits of financial security."

screen of logic: the filter or gate that stands between the conscious and subconscious minds; determines if new information is worthy to enter and be stored with existing information we use to make decisions and value

Glossary of Terms 33

judgements. "Bob has so trained himself to fail that his *screen of logic* now filters out any positive images he develops of himself."

self-discipline: a system or process of evaluating one's goals, plans, attitudes, habits, and moral values and establishing a set of standards to be followed without input or undue pressure from others. "The person who has developed *self-discipline* does not have to be encouraged by others to succeed."

self-confidence: the belief in self achieved through trial and error and other personal qualities that enable a person to be successful at chosen tasks. "You can tell he had a lot of *self-confidence* just by the calm and assured way he walked."

"sovereign citizen" concept: the idea that the government officially recognizes the individual as the source of ultimate power; manifested both politically and economically when citizens have the freedom to choose their destinies. "The United States of America is based on the *sovereign citizen* concept—the people are the real source of governmental power."

stagnation: a condition or state with little or no movement; the absence of personal growth. "The president's failure to develop new ideas caused a real case of *stagnation* for the company."

subconscious mind: that portion of the human mind where knowledge and information is stored; the mental bank that produces on demand decisions, value judgements, ideas, and all forms of personal communications. "I sensed that the solution was hidden in my *subconscious mind*, but I couldn't find it."

success: most generally speaking, the ability to live life in one's own way; in today's society, however, also includes a positive measure of financial security or independence.

"True and long-lasting *success* yields genuine satisfaction, but that success must be earned."

tangible: able to be seen and touched. Tangible rewards include money, property, stocks, bonds, and other visible forms of wealth. "That she had done well financially was evidenced by her many *tangible* possessions."

traditional values: spiritual, moral, and social norms that became a part of our culture in the early days of our nation's history; include marriage, the home, family, church, the work ethic, and so forth. "Sam was a staunch advocate of *traditional values* who manifested his commitment in the way he lived."

value: the degree of emotional and mental attachment a person has for another person, place or thing; often expressed in terms of money; in an economic sense, the specific outcome of the law of supply and demand. "John had developed a sound *value* system based on truth, honesty, and hard work."

verbal communication: the spoken word; transmission of ideas and concepts to others in either a formal or informal manner using speech. (While *verbal* often means "having to do with words," I would like to emphasize the sense "spoken out loud.") "The proof that Ellen had great *verbal communication* skills could be shown by the fact that she could say more in less time than anyone else I knew."

worth: the quality something has that renders it desirable or valuable; can be increased or decreased by instituting changes of various kinds. "The *worth* of a pine tree is increased when it is changed into a useful article of furniture."

Part One

Who Am I?

Who am I? I'm a very special, unique person because God is not in the business of making junk.

CHAPTER 1

A New Beginning

Congratulations on your decision to read this book. Before we get seriously underway, however, there are three basic questions I want to ask you to consider. First, *why did you pick up this book and start reading it?* Your answer to this question could mean a great deal in terms of the benefits you will receive for the time you are investing.

If you purchased this book because you felt the need to develop and use more of your latent potential, and you would like to be happier and more successful, congratulations again! In time, I know you will be richly rewarded for your investment. If your answer is along the lines of "I received it as a gift from a friend," or "I thought it might be interesting, so I checked it out of the library or resource center," or "I'm studying this book as a part of a course in my school or college," then you will have to decide as we go along as to the benefits you want to receive from it.

Here is my second question: As these thoughts begin to enter your mind, *where are you* in terms of age, education, attitude, and past achievements? A young person still in high school, trying to make some decisions regarding a career choice and to establish short- and long-term goals will certainly view this book in a different light than the person who has finished college, has a fantastic career, a nice home, and a family, and is now planning for long-range financial security.

Another interesting contrast takes into account the opinion a person has about self. One person perhaps has a positive mental attitude, looks at life and the future optimistically, possesses a high degree of self-confidence, and knows how to go about getting what he or she wants. On the other hand is the person who, because of a poor environment or past failures and mistakes, has a very negative mental attitude and a poor self-image, who generally views life and the future with pessimism. This person often has the deep-down feeling that success is for other people, not for "a loser like me."

There is also the issue of past achievements. If you are already sucessful, you have developed what I call a "success momentum." You will keep getting more successful because you will keep doing what it takes to be a success. Compare this with the person who has never had encouragement, faith, or instruction from anyone on how to become a success. As a result, that person can develop a "failure momentum" that fosters nothing but more failure. When it comes to really enjoying life with its many rewards, unfortunately, the person with "failure momentum" is living in reverse.

As you think about your answer to my second question, you should at least establish a foundation toward understanding some of the filters in your mind through which information in this book will pass.

My third question to you is this: when it comes to making life-changing decisions and choices, *who will you believe?* In other words, what are the sources of information you are using as the foundation upon which your life and your future will be built? From a very practical standpoint, we know that most of the information that comes to us on a day-to-day basis is not all that important with regard to making our most critical life-changing decisions. However, there are times when we must make decisions that will drastically affect our long-range success and happiness. When we become adults, most of us are given the freedom to choose. We can choose where we will live, whether or not we will get married and if so, to whom, what kind of career, job, or line of work we wish to go into, and many other far-reaching decisions of this nature. There may also be other potentially life-changing decisions we have to make. For example, someone may ask you to help plan and carry out a bank robbery, or be unfaithful to your spouse. Decisions of this nature can often result in negative consequences.

When it comes to having access to the right information that will help you make those critical, life-changing decisions, *who will you believe?* Please look deeply into your subconscious mind. Would you believe your parents? Would you believe your teachers? Would you believe the great philosophers of the past; men like Confucius, Socrates, Aristotle, or Plato? Would you believe men and women of more recent times who have achieved outstanding success like Abraham Lincoln, Will Rogers, Margaret Mead, Albert Einstein, Henry Ford, Susan B. Anthony, Martin Luther King, Billy Graham, Pearl Buck, or Harry Truman? I am sure that you realize I could add thousands of people to this list. I could also ask whether you will believe those who you see and hear on television, on the radio, in newspapers, and in other means of communication, including all the books and magazines now in print.

So again, in light of what I have just said, I ask my third question. When it comes to making critical, life-changing decisions, *who will you believe?* It is really something to think about, isn't it? I hope we can mutually agree (regardless of who said it in the past) that unless we are building our lives and futures based on truth, we are building on sand, and nothing of it will stand. So truth is what we should all seek if we want to be successful and happy over the long haul. Do you agree?

From a personal standpoint, if someone were to ask me, "Jim, who will you believe?," I would say, "I've always believed the Bible to be the primary source of truth." Whether you concur or not, I can at least say that it has withstood the test of time. My purpose in making this statement is not to place a religious emphasis on this book, because I believe in personal freedoms. Every person in America should be free to make personal choices for himself or herself. As the author of this book, however, I want to state very clearly that I believe in an almighty God and therefore that I believe in the Bible. In this book, I will discuss your spiritual life, but I will not make reference to a specific church, denomination, or doctrine because this is a very personal and private area of your life. My point is only that you must have some standard upon which you can answer the question "Who will you believe?"

With these three questions behind us, if you are ready, let's begin an exciting journey together. I hope you will get so emotionally involved in reading this book that it will almost be like reading a novel. The difference is that you will be learning and benefitting from the ideas it contains as we go along. After all, this book is about the most important person in the world—it is about *you*, your life, your plans, your goals, your dreams, and your future. I am committed to helping you plan your life and pursue your goals until that day comes when you can look back and say, "Jim, I never dreamt in my wildest imagination that life could be so much fun, so rewarding, and so fulfilling. I eagerly look forward to each new day."

Here then is the logical place to begin to develop a plan for your life and your future. I want to help you realize, in case you have not already come to this conclusion, that you are a very special, unique person, unlike any other person who has ever lived. You might wonder if this is really true. How do you know that you are special? I know that it is true for two very valid reasons. First, do you remember what I said earlier about a standard for believing? The Bible says in the book of Genesis that we are created in the image of God. Because we are God's special creation each one of us is unique and very special. I also know personal uniqueness is a fact from a scientific standpoint. Science has proven, beyond a shadow of a doubt, that no two human beings are exactly alike. For example, we know that no two people have exactly the same fingerprints or footprints.

From this moment on, I hope you will begin to see yourself as you have perhaps never seen yourself before—a one-of-a-kind, very special, unique person. Regardless of your position and station in life, whether you are young or old, male or female, rich or poor, whether you are educated or uneducated, a success or failure, you are nevertheless unique. Since God created you, God loves you, a fact that makes you a very special person. Please, please, never forget this. It is central to many of the concepts I will be presenting throughout this entire book. If you do not believe in your own uniqueness and worth, you are needlessly holding yourself back. (If you have a poor self-image, I'll tell you in the next chapter what you can do about it.)

I would like for you to read the following poem about "the one and only you." I believe the message here will help you see what I have been trying to get across.

The One and Only You

Every single blade of grass
And every flake of snow
Are just a wee bit different
There's no two alike, you know.

From something small like grains of sand
To each gigantic star
Each one was made with this in mind—
To be just what they are.

How foolish then to imitate,
How useless to pretend
When each one of us comes from a mind
Whose ideas never end.

> There will only be just one of me
> To show what I can do.
> And likewise, you should feel very proud
> There's only one of *you*.

Now, please answer the question at hand truthfully. *Who am I?* Your answer here is a reflection of your current self-image and how you see yourself!

CHAPTER 2

Self-Image: How It Controls Your Life

I hope you are excited about the tremendous amount of potential you possess. You should know beyond the shadow of a doubt that you are a very special and unique person. If you recall, I have said that your answer to the question "Who am I?" is a reflection of your current self-image and how you see yourself. Whether you believe it or not, this is a true statement. What I want to do now is discuss the power of your self-image and how it does control your life.

I realize the possibility is good that you already know a great deal about self-image. If you do, so much the better—the things I say here will simply reinforce what is already clear to you. There are, however, millions and millions of people who know very little about self-image and how it literally controls their lives day after day. The reason many people do not know much about self-image is because its discovery was made in recent years. It therefore has not been taught to any great degree in our nation's educational system. All of this is true even though the discovery of the influence of self-image has been called the most important psychological breakthrough of the century!

To go one step further, many people know about self-image in a general sense, but do not possess an in-depth

"I know my self-image controls my life and I'm going to make it consistent with the person I really want to be."

understanding of what it is, how it was discovered, how it works for or against a person. Still more important, many people do not know how to go about changing a poor self-image. Self-image has been called a life-governing mechanism, which simply means you cannot rise above the limits that it imposes. Please allow me to explain this.

Self-image works somewhat like a governor on a motorized vehicle. The governor is a device to limit the vehicle's speed. Imagine you are driving a school bus down one of those flat Texas highways with a governor on your bus set at fifty miles per hour. You could press the accelerator all the way to the floor, but the bus would not go any faster than fifty miles per hour, because that is where the governor is set. The only way you could travel any faster would be to advance the setting. This principle also applies to your self-image. You cannot go any higher, travel any faster, or become any more successful that the current limits of your self-image. This is why self-image is called a life-governing mechanism.

From this point forward, as I continue to discuss self-image, you must realize that your greatest potentials for growth, success, happiness, more income, and all the important things you desire in your life will only come to you within the bounds of your dominant self-image. In my opinion, developing a realistic plan to improve your self-image will produce more results than anything else you could do to invest your time.

There is something else for you to consider. All of the ideas and concepts you encounter in this book, you will view in light of your current self-image. If your self-image is healthy, positive, and good, these ideas will help you even more. If your self-image is negative and poor, these ideas will simply be for "the other person." They will not be for you, unless you are willing to accept the challenge of changing your self-image.

Now, in a systematic fashion, let us examine the self-image: what it is, how it was discovered, how it works to control our lives, and how we can change or improve a self-image that limits success and growth. Self-image in a general sense is the mental picture you have of yourself. This mental picture not only takes in what you see when you look into a mirror, it is also how you feel about what you see inside where the reflective power of a mirror cannot penetrate.

It is interesting that the discovery of self-image came about as a result of work in the field of plastic surgery. Many people have been involved, but the most notable is the late Dr. Maxwell Maltz, author of the best-seller *Psychocybernetics*.

In the late 1940s and early to mid 1950s, Dr. Maltz began his practice of plastic or cosmetic surgery on the West Coast. He developed a new surgical technique to work with patients who had unbecoming features, scars, or deformities and transform them into much more physically attractive people. As time passed, Dr. Maltz began to observe amazing changes in the lives of some of his patients. Many who came to him were shy, reserved, unhappy, and failing in life, simply because they did not like what they saw when they looked in the mirror. However, after plastic surgery, they often made startling changes for the better. Many of his patients became more outgoing, developed pleasing personalities, and began to acquire levels of self-confidence they once believed impossible.

People's lives changed because they went from ugliness to attractiveness. Sounds simple, doesn't it? In the course of his work, however, Dr. Maltz discovered something else that has literally transformed thousands of people's lives for the better in the past thirty to forty years. After several months, some of Dr. Maltz's patients came back to him and said, "Dr. Maltz, I look attractive, but I still feel ugly." It was at this point that Dr. Maltz began to realize that self-image, how we see ourselves, is deeper than the skin. It is also how we feel about ourselves inside, where we must live. (Does this information give you some additional insight into your own self-image? I truly think that it should!)

In addition to the discovery that self-image is more than skin deep, Dr. Maltz also discovered how people could change or improve for the better (and that, by today's standards, is real news!) Here is how it works. People who have good self-images and are successful are called winners. Winners are in the habit of doing things that winners are supposed to do. They have the real-life experiences on a regular basis that tend to reinforce and build up "winner" self-images. On the other hand, losers in life, those with poor self-images, do not have positive real-life experiences. While conducting his research, Dr. Maltz found that losers in life could change self-image through a process of synthetic experience. They could, in essence, create those winning experiences in their minds with the same effect as if it were happening in real life.

My friend, do you realize what this means? In your mind you must see yourself as being more successful before it will actually come to pass. This is the process of synthetic experience.

If you feel the need to change or improve your self-image, there are positive steps you can take. Decide what kind of person you would like to become, and think about the qualities you would need to become like that. Begin to hold these thoughts of yourself in your mind on a regular and consistent basis, and before long, you will also begin to feel like this new and better person. When you can see and feel an objective, it is just a matter of time until you get there.

Here is an easy and effective plan you can follow to bring about a change in your self-image. First, write a clear description of the person you would like to become on an index card. Carry it with you and look at it often. Slowly but surely, you will notice little changes in your life for the better. The second step is to remember that you are a very special, unique person, the "one and only you." You have latent talents and abilities just waiting to be developed and utilized. The third point concerns your relationships with others. Generally, you get back from others what you first give to them. If you treat others as important, worthwhile people, they will in turn treat you the same way. This will make you feel better about yourself and that will enhance your self-image. Fourth, you must begin thinking about goals. If you do not already have written, specific goals, begin to think about those things you would like to have and what you would like to be. If your self-image is low, your goals will be low. Your goals must conform to your self-image. That is why it is called a life-governing mechanism. The better your self-image becomes, the higher the goals will be that you will set and reach.

The One in the Mirror

As you go through life in your struggle for self
And the world makes you king or queen for a day,
Just go to the mirror and look at yourself,
And see what that person has to say.
For it isn't your mother or father or spouse
Whose judgement upon you must pass;
But the one whose verdict means most in your life
Is the one staring back in the glass.
He is the one to please, never mind the rest,
For he is with you right up to the end,
And you have passed your most dangerous, difficult
    task
If the one in the glass is your friend.
You may be like Jack Horner and chisel a plum
And think you're a wonderful gal or guy,
But the one in the glass thinks you're only a bum
If you can't look him square in the eye.
You may fool the whole world down the pathway of
    years
And get slaps on the back as you pass.

But your final reward will be heartaches and tears,
If you've cheated the one in the glass.

Please answer my question again for yourself. Really and truly, who am I?

"It's important to have goals to strive for, because you can't be a winner in life without them."

CHAPTER 3

Why Goals Are Important for You

Research in the field of human development has proven that only five percent of all working people in America have specific, written goals and can tell you what they are working toward at any given time. What about you? At this point in your life, do you have specific, written goals that you are working to achieve?

If you do have goals, congratulations! You are definitely in the top five percent. If you do not have specific, written goals, you can probably give good reasons why you do not— but good excuses won't help you get where you are going. I want you to see that it is necessary for you to have goals if you want to achieve success. I've discovered that many people do not set goals simply because they have never had anyone take time to explain why goals are really necessary.

Let's go back for a moment and look at the process of goal-setting from an historical perspective. In the earliest days of our nation's history, approximately ninety-five percent of all people lived and worked on the farm, where practically all of their total needs were produced. Because of the nature of farming, goals were not really important back then. The seasons of the year told the farmer when it was time to plow, to plant, and to harvest. Goals were not really necessary.

Another important historical consideration is that high schools in this country were originally structured to prepare students to enter college. Not too many years ago a person who had a college degree (a doctor, lawyer, engineer, or teacher) was automatically considered to be a success, primarily because the demand for educated people was greater than the supply.

As we look back into the more recent past, say fifty years ago, goals were still not very important, because our society was no where near as complex as it is today. Life was simple and moved at a much slower pace.

Something happened, however, that gave personal goals the importance they have in today's times. Agricultural society gradually gave way to industrial society, and that changed to our modern informational society. While this social transformation was happening, the percentage of products and services individuals produce personally to meet their own needs was reversed. Our forefathers produced ninety-five percent of their total needs; we now purchase ninety-five percent of our needs from others. This means that time has now become money.

As society changed and more jobs and careers opened up, the clear-cut choices for a person's life and career path became washed away. Since the youth of today have no farm to go back to, and since there are over fifty thousand job possibilities, the selection of a job or career has become a very complicated and often fearful process. As a result of this dilemma, it is reported that up to seventy percent of all working people are bored and unhappy with their jobs. When the "new" wears off of a new job, most people become bored—which means they have no great motivating idea or goal. On the other hand, if you have written, specific goals that you are working to achieve, you will not be bored, you will be excited about each new day.

Here's an example to illustrate my point; in your mind, picture a rushing river, and then a placid lake. Can you see the two? Now which would become stagnant first? Of course, the correct answer is the lake. The river is moving, the lake is not. Another way to look at it is that the river is going somewhere, but the lake is standing still. People's lives are much the same way. Those who have goals are moving, while people who have no goals become bored and stagnant.

An important reason why you should have specific, written goals to strive for is that you cannot hit a target you cannot see. For you not to have written goals to look at often could be compared to putting a blindfold on you, placing a gun in your hand, turning you around several times, and saying, "There's a target not too far away. Let's see if you can hit it." In most cases you cannot hit a target you cannot see. True?

The people in our society who are the real winners in life are goal-setters. They make up their minds what they want and then go after it.

In conclusion, here are very good reasons why goals are necessary:

- You cannot be a winner in the game of life without specific, realistic, attainable goals.
- Goals are necessary to motivate you to develop your latent potential.
- Human beings are goal-seeking organisms. They are happier and more fulfilled when working toward something definite.
- Achievement of goals is necessary to develop a good self-image, a positive mental attitude, and a high degree of self-confidence.
- Goals will help you evaluate your priorities and maintain a balanced life.

Part One: Review

I have read the three chapters covering the question "Who am I?"

☐ I have a better understanding of why I am a very special, unique person.

☐ I have a better understanding of the power of my self-image and how it literally controls my life.

☐ I understand more fully why it is important to have specific, written goals to strive for.

If you cannot affirm each of these statements by checking the boxes, please go back and reread these chapters before proceeding.

FOOD FOR THOUGHT

"No goals"—Men and rivers are both made crooked by following the path of least resistance.

Part Two

Where Am I?

"Thanks for these priceless gifts. I will use them to develop and enhance my talents and abilities to make my life a success!"

CHAPTER 4

Time for a Check-Up: Your Personal Inventory

In Chapter 1, I asked an important question. "Where are you in terms of age, education, attitude and past achievements?" What I want to share with you now will be greatly affected by your answer to that question. If you are a young person, just starting out and making plans for your future, you will have a different attitude and a somewhat different approach from the person who is middle aged or even retired, and wants to continue to grow mentally. (I am sure you know it is better to wear out than to rust out!)

At this point, I would like to offer a word of caution for young people reading this book. I find many young people are very idealistic and very self-assured. That is good, but quite often young people think they have all or at least most of the answers. It is only after several years of living with some of life's frustrations, heartaches, and disappointments that they are receptive to ideas from others. On the other hand, the person who has been out in the real world for some time is often looking for new ideas, suggestions, and life-changing concepts to help make the most of remaining time. I realize these are things that could have been left unsaid, but all too often, we assume people know things that they do not—or sometimes they know things but do not think of them. Isn't this true?

With these thoughts in mind, I want you to consider your future by taking a personal inventory. Let's see exactly where you are at this point in time. In most cases, it is impossible to develop a plan to get where you want to go unless you first determine where you are now. By taking time for a check-up in your own life now, you should have a better understanding of what talents and resources you have available as you plan for your future. As you take inventory of your present condition, stay on the positive side of self-evaluation. Your message to yourself should be affirming: "I have time, I have unique talents and abilities, and I have the opportunity to develop and use them. What I do with these priceless assets in the future is for the most part up to me. It's my future, and I'm going to make the most of it!"

Once you have a fairly accurate understanding of where you are now, developing a plan for your future will be much easier. That is what we will be doing from this point to the end of the book. Remember that this book is about the most important person in the world; it is about *you* and your future.

Please fill in the following exercise as accurately and honestly as you can. Take a little time and think about your responses. When you complete this exercise, you should be able to see that you have a lot more going for you than you may have realized.

Personal Assessment

My name is _____
and I am a special, unique person. I live in the State of _____.
My home address is _____.
My business or school address is _____
_____.

Age: _____ Education completed: _____

Other courses completed: _____
Other achievements: _____
Organizations to which I belong: _____

Offices held (past or present): _____

Awards received: _____
Special talents developed: _____
Things I like to do best (work and hobbies): __

My strong points: _____
Points I need to improve: _____

Build on your strong points. They offer you the best road to success. Recognize the areas in which you need to improve, but do not get discouraged. Commit yourself to improving them one at a time.

There is more to the personal inventory you need to take. One of the most important personal qualities you will need to develop to reach your goals is the ability to cause others to like you. We are all in the "people business." The following test will give you some indication of your proficiency in this area. (Answer each question by writing "yes" or "no" at the end of the line.)

MY RELATIONS WITH OTHERS

1. If you make a promise, do you always keep it?_____
2. If someone—a friend, co-worker or member of your family—is in need of help, do you give that help cheerfully?_____
3. Are you frequently witty in a sarcastic way?_____

4. Do you have a tendency to gain attention by "topping" the remark made by the previous speaker in a conversation?_____
5. Are you usually ill at ease with strangers?_____
6. Are you critical of others when you feel they are at fault?_____
7. Can you usually avoid being bossy?_____
8. Are you able to avoid ridiculing other people when they are not present?_____
9. Do you frequently laugh at the mistakes of others?_____
10. When others make mistakes (in fact, in grammar, in pronunciation) do you correct them?_____
11. Do you smile easily?_____
12. Are you able to praise and compliment other people easily?_____
13. Do you frequently try to reform other people?_____
14. Are you able to keep your personal troubles to yourself?_____
15. Are you suspicious of other people's motives?_____
16. Do you frequently borrow the belongings of others?_____
17. Do you enjoy gossip?_____
18. Are you able to keep out of other people's business most of the time?_____
19. Do you avoid talking about yourself, your belongings or your successes most of the time?_____
20. Do you ever use belittling words when referring to those who differ from you in religion, race, politics, or beliefs?_____

Now, let's score this exercise to discover if you have the abilities that cause others to like you. Give yourself five points each for "yes" answers to questions 1, 2, 7, 8, 11, 12, 14, 18, or 19. "No" answers to questions 3, 4, 5, 6, 9, 10, 13, 15, 16, 17, or 20 are worth five points each. If your total score is below seventy, perhaps you are turning people off.

FOOD FOR THOUGHT:

You are a very special, unique person.
Please never forget this!

"GIGO—'Garbage in, garbage out.' What goes into my mind will sooner or later come out in my life."

CHAPTER 5

The Human Mind and How It Functions

Do you look at your future with hope and optimism or do you feel defeated and discouraged a good part of the time? How you answer this question will tell you a lot about your mind and your habits. I want to share some information about the mind and how it functions, but first I want to tell you something that you may either accept or reject at this time.

Remember my earlier question, "Who do you believe?" How you have used your mind in the past is responsible for most of your present circumstances, achievements, and failures, in addition to determining whether or not you have been able to solve most of your problems. If you have permitted your problems to completely decimate you, there is something I want you to see. What happens to you in the future will depend to a large degree on your understanding of how your mind functions and how you can develop and use your mind to achieve those goals you want to achieve.

Now I realize that I have made some pretty positive statements about what you can do. Depending on your knowledge of mental functions and the confidence you have in yourself, you may agree with me completely or you may doubt what I have said. At this point, however, I would like to discuss some of the basic concepts concerning the human mind and why most of us fail to use its great potential.

Let's begin by using the example of a newborn baby boy, with all of the potential for success and greatness in the world. Almost from the moment of birth, the baby's development begins. He puts on weight and increases in size because he is being nourished.

In addition to the baby's physical development, which we can see, he also begins the process of mental development, which we cannot see. Inside the baby's head is a brain. Medical science has determined that a human brain consists of three major parts; the cerebrum, cerebellum, and medulla oblongata. Different parts of the brain are responsible for various functions of the body. The brain is the nerve center or control mechanism for every bodily function.

Connected in some way to the brain is the human mind— the arena in which ideas are stored and manipulated. A new baby comes into the world with so-called natural instincts, but his mind could be compared to an empty cardboard box (the key word here is "empty"). As the baby grows and develops, the sights and sounds in the home environment begin to filter in through one or more of the five senses. Later in school, teachers strive to add more knowledge to the "empty cardboard box" by teaching basic skills such as reading, writing, and arithmetic.

What is our newborn baby, who has now become a school-aged youngster, to do with the information he receives? He obviously must devise some method or system to make decisions. This is where value judgements enter the process. Our school-aged youngster must now begin to use his acquired knowledge to decide what is right and what is wrong, what is good and what is bad.

Do you see the relevance of this example for your own situation? Are you beginning to have a better understanding of those forces and influences that have shaped your life or filled your "empty cardboard box"?

The human mind has two parts, the conscious mind and the subconscious mind. The conscious mind is the part we might refer to as "up-front," which only receives new information that comes along when it is alert and awake. The subconscious mind, on the other hand, is the warehouse where knowledge and information are stored. When information is properly stored in our subconscious minds, it can be recalled for later use and combined with other information to make decisions and value judgements.

Have you ever stopped to consider how information gets into your subconscious mind? In my example of the newborn baby, I said that information comes into his mind through one or more of the five senses. This is true, and apart from subliminal learning, the information only comes into the conscious mind. At this point, it is not part of the baby's knowledge. It only becomes knowledge as it passes to the subconscious mind to be stored.

Information is transferred from the conscious mind to the subconscious in two basic ways. The first is repetition, such as the process of memorization, in which material is studied over and over until it is etched into memory. Secondly, some information goes into the subconscious mind with the aid of impact and strong emotion. For example, if you are an older adult, you can probably remember what you were doing the exact moment you heard that President John F. Kennedy had been shot.

I hope I have done a good job of making your thoughts clear on this point. I want to capitalize on what I have said by sharing several basic concepts that could mean the difference for you between success and failure, happiness and unhappiness.

When information passes from your conscious mind to your subconscious mind, it will encounter a mechanism that I call the "screen of logic." The screen of logic is somewhat like a guard that stands between the conscious and the subconscious. When new information approaches the guard, a quick review of all information stored in your subconscious mind is made. If the new information compares favorably to the data established in the subconscious, that is, if it appears to be logical or true, it is permitted to enter. On the other hand, if the new information does not compare favorably, it is rejected. Have you any idea what this means for you personally?

For example, if I told you that in the next five years you were going to become an outstanding success in your field, you would either accept the statement as true or reject it as foolish or empty talk. Your acceptance or rejection would be based on what is already in your subconscious mind. It is very important to understand this: what you have in your subconscious mind right now is what you are using as a basis to make your decisions and value judgements.

The mind functions somewhat like a computer. What is programmed into the mind sooner or later will be expressed in actions, speech, and feelings. You may be familiar with the computer term GIGO—"garbage in, garbage out." What you feed your mind—what you permit to enter—is what comes out in your life.

Ask yourself this question: "If I am not as happy and successful as I would like to be, could it be that I have not been as selective as I should have been in what I have permitted to enter my subconscious mind?" It's something to think about, isn't it?

Your mind has the potential to function as a machine that serves you, much like what engineers call a servomechanism. Here is how this works: If you recall, I have said that human beings are goal-seeking organisms. We tend to be happier and more fulfilled when we are working toward specific, written goals. By deciding in advance what your goals are, by writing them down on paper and looking at them often, you will be using the process of repetition to drive them deeper into your subconscious mind. (That is, of course, if your goals are able to pass through the screen of logic in order to be stored.) Once your goals are stored deep in your subconscious mind, your mind takes over—like a servomechanism—to help you reach them.

Here is an example to demonstrate how it works. A batter hits a high fly ball, and the right fielder sees catching the ball as his goal. His mind acts as a servomechanism and directs his feet, step by step, until he is in the exact spot where the ball will come down. When he is in position, he simply catches the ball. The sequence of events may seem routine, but it is not. It is really a miracle. What is important for you to understand is that your mind, acting as a servomechanism, will direct you to reach any goal you set. All that you have to do is stay with your goals, and avoid confusing yourself by setting mutually incompatible or unattainable goals. Your servomechanism won't function if you tell it to catch two or three fly balls at the same time!

Above all, I want you to see how valuable and important your mind really is. If you will feed it the right information, you will greatly enhance your success. One specific thing you can do to cultivate your mind is to be very selective in associating with people who will inspire you. Remember, birds of a feather flock together. If you spend time with successful people, you will begin to train your mind in success attitudes.

List six successful people with whom you would like to associate, who would serve as good role models.

1. _____
2. _____
3. _____
4. _____
5. _____
6. _____

List three self-improvement books that will help set your mind on a positive course.

1. _____
2. _____
3. _____

FOOD FOR THOUGHT:

The Optimist's Creed

Promise Yourself:

To be so strong that nothing can disturb your peace of mind.

To talk health, happiness, and prosperity to every person you meet.

To make all your friends feel that they are valuable individuals.

To look at the sunny side of everything and make your optimism come true.

To think only of the best, to work only for the best, and to expect only the best.

To be just as enthusiastic about the successes of others as you are about your own.

To forget the mistakes of the past and press on to the greater achievements of the future.

To wear a cheerful countenance at all times and give every living creature you meet a smile.

To give so much time to the improving of yourself that you have no time to criticize others.

To be too large for worry, too noble for anger, too strong for fear, and too happy to permit the presence of trouble.

CHAPTER 6

Your Greatest Power: The Power to Choose

It has been said that mankind's greatest enemy is ignorance. Even in the climate of freedom here in America, we are enslaved to the degree that we remain ignorant. It is my hope that you are beginning to feel a new sense of freedom and power to take control of your life, and are becoming the person you are capable of becoming. While many people in our society are happy and content just the way they are, many others yearn to be more successful and to experience a deeper purpose and meaning in life.

If you do want to move forward in life, it is critically important for you to see that your greatest power is the power you have to choose and make right decisions. Almost from the moment human beings come into the world, and certainly later in life as we pass through our teenage years into adulthood, our lives are made up of one decision after another. A human life can be accurately described as a continuous series of decisions, interrupted only by the period of inactivity called "sleep."

The issue of personal success in life really revolves around whether or not the right decisions have been made most of the time. Do you agree? This is more the case in America than

"Whatever choices I make in life, I must be prepared to live with the consequences."

anywhere else in the world, because we are free to make most of the fateful decisions that affect our lives.

At this point, I want to pose a question. If personal success and happiness depends on making the right decisions most of the time, why do we see so many people who are discouraged, disillusioned, frustrated, and failing in life? Could it be because they have made the wrong choices or decisions too often?

The reason that explains why most people fail is procrastination. Too often people put off making fateful decisions until they are forced to, and by then, quite often, it is too late.

There are several matters that account for procrastination. One of the most basic needs of human beings is the need for security. To achieve security, people try to "play it safe." Many people will not act or make decisions at all for fear they will fail. This problem can be made even worse by problems with self-image. A poor self-image or lack of self-confidence causes many people to put off making life-changing decisions.

Perhaps most important is the role of the subconscious mind in decision making. If the subconscious is filled with more negative information than positive information, the fear of failure can overcome the desire for gain. There is an antidote for this difficulty that can get you back on the track of successful decision making. Please consider that fear can be nothing more than "FEAR"—False Evidence Appearing Real. If you look at the facts carefully, your reasons for fear will often evaporate.

If you have problems making decisions, there is a definite method you can follow that will help you make right decisions most of the time. Remember that I do not—and cannot—guarantee one-hundred percent results. If you do anything at all, you are bound to make some mistakes. The goal is to make careful and timely decisions and learn from the mistakes you do make.

HOW TO MAKE DECISIONS

1. Define the problem. A problem well stated is a problem half solved.
2. Get all the facts you can about the problem.
3. Consider as many possible solutions as you can develop. A brainstorming session with two or more people might be helpful.
4. Evaluate what you think the consequences will be of each possible solution.
5. Make your decision based on the true facts and your prospects for success will be greatly enhanced.
6. Make your decision now; do not put it off.
7. Be prepared to live with the consequences.

As you read and re-read this book, I hope you will come back to this chapter often. It can make a difference in your future by building your decision-making skills.

One of the real problems in making decisions is that we will usually do something because we feel like doing it, not necessarily because it is right or best for us. We try to justify our actions later. "I did it because..." usually turns out to be a lame justification. Another problem that affects our lives that is related to making decisions is worry. I'm not sure if you realize it, but worry often paralyzes decision-making before it gets started. The pity is that worry is often purposeless.

Do You Act or React?

I walked with my friend, a Quaker, to the newsstand the other night, and he bought a paper, thanking the newsie politely. The newsie didn't even acknowledge it.

"A sullen fellow, isn't he?" I commented.

"Oh, he's that way every night," shrugged my friend.

"Then why do you continue to be so polite to him?" I asked.

"Why not?" inquired my friend. "Why should I let him decide how I am going to act?"

As I thought about this incident later, it occurred to me that the most important word was *act*. My friend *acts* toward people; most of us *react* toward them.

He has a sense of inner balance which is lacking in most of us; he knows who he is, what he stands for, and how he should behave. He refuses to return incivility for incivility, because then he would no longer be in command of his own conduct.

We interpret the command in the Bible to return good for evil as a moral injunction, which it is. But it is also a psychological prescription for our emotional health.

Nobody is unhappier than the perpetual reactor. His center of emotional gravity is not rooted within himself, where it belongs, but in the world outside him. His spiritual temperature is always being raised or lowered by the social climate around him, and he is a creature at the mercy of these elements.

Praise gives him a feeling of euphoria, which is false, because it does not last and it does not come from self-approval. Criticism depresses him more than it should, because it confirms his own secretly shaky opinion of himself. Snubs hurt him, and the merest suspicion of unpopularity in any quarter rouses him to bitterness.

A serenity of spirit cannot be achieved until we become the masters of our own actions and attitudes. To let others determine whether we shall be rude or gracious, elated or depressed, is to relinquish control over our own personalities, which are ultimately all we possess. The only true possession is self-possession.

Worry Table

Things that never happen	40 percent
Things that cannot be changed by all the worry in the world	35 percent
Things that turn out other than expected	15 percent
Petty, useless worries	8 percent
Legitimate worries	2 percent
	100 percent

How many people do you know personally who fail to make proper decisions or ruin their health because of worry? My "Worry Table" is designed to show that the odds are fifty to one against the worries you have being worth real concern.

The processes involved in making decisions and worrying are really learned habits. When you put off making decisions or worry about needless things for long periods of time, you are actually forming dangerous habits—procrastination or worry. If you are to overcome procrastination or worry, you must put new information in your subconscious mind to change your thought patterns. To say it another way, your desire for gain must be greater than your fear of loss. To be sure, life is to be lived in forward gear, not in reverse or neutral.

The greatest power you have is the power to choose and make the right decisions. Generally speaking, when you have no high goals to strive for, it usually means you have no motivation or reason to make important decisions. W. Clement Stone, a highly successful business executive, has as his motto, "Do it now." Immediate action is a great habit to develop once you have made the proper decisions.

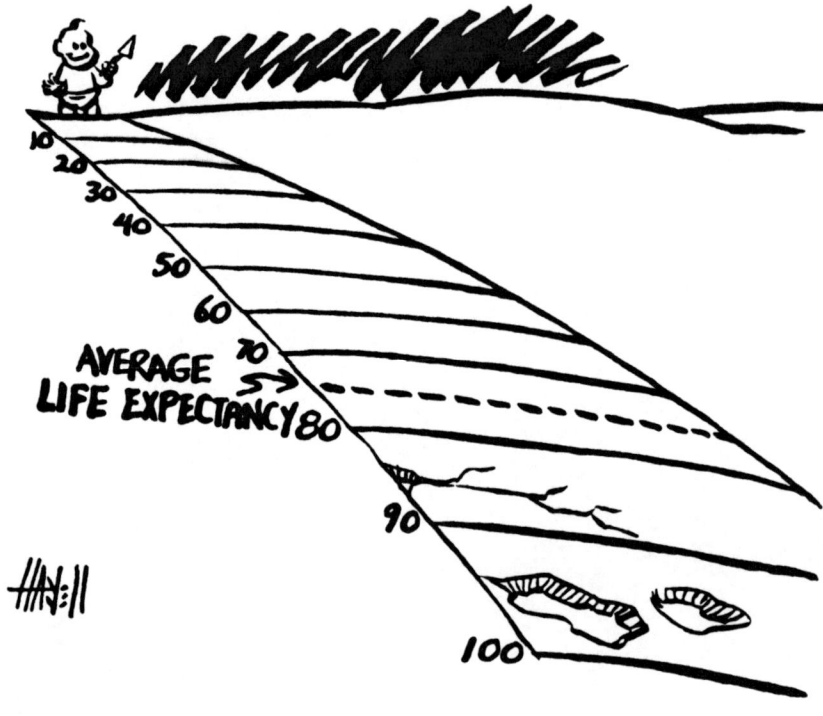

"My future is looking great, but I know I must take care of my health to have long-term success and happiness."

CHAPTER 7

Good Health: The Key to Long-Lasting Success

Sometime ago, a television commercial featured the slogan: "When you've got your health, you've got just about everything." I hope you have already come to the conclusion that having good health is one of the greatest blessings a human being can experience. I firmly believe that maintaining and preserving health is the key to long-lasting success and happiness.

I am aware that many people are born with disabling handicaps and diseases of various kinds, while thousands of other people are stricken later in life. If by chance this is your plight, I truly have compassion for you. I hope you are receiving all the support and help you need and deserve.

There are, however, many people who have had physical handicaps of one kind or another but who were still blessed with sound minds. Some of these people rank among the greatest success stories of all times. The names Helen Keller, Franklin D. Roosevelt, Ray Charles, and Joni Eareckson remind us of only a few of the thousands of people who have not let handicaps keep them from becoming successful.

I cannot stress too much the importance of taking good care of yourself. Unless you are willing to apply some common sense practices to take care of your health, the success you seek may be short lived. You may not be around to enjoy those things for which you have worked. If you are middle-aged, you know that health *is* "just about everything." If you are younger, I hope you will trust my advice and pay careful attention to how you treat yourself from now on.

To help you maintain and preserve your health, one sensible matter is to have physical examinations done regularly. If you have not had a medical checkup recently, go to your doctor for a thorough examination. In performing the exam, your doctor will usually check a number of signs that indicate the status of your health.

- your temperature: Normal is 98.6 F, though there is some variation between individuals. A higher reading usually indicates some type of infection in your body.

- your pulse: Normal for most people is about seventy-two beats per minute. This will vary, depending upon your age, sex, and physical condition; it ranges from fifty to ninety beats per minute. A well-conditioned heart returns to normal very quickly after periods of exercise.

- your blood pressure: Usually the doctor will take a pressure reading from vessels in your upper arm. Two readings are taken during the examination: one is a higher pressure called the systolic pressure which occurs when the heart contracts; the lowest pressure, which represents the heart muscle at rest, is called the diastolic pressure. The average person for adults under age forty is about one hundred twenty for the systolic and eighty for the diastolic. Your blood pressure tells the doctor a number of things about the condition of your health. Since many deaths in the United States result from heart attacks and strokes, a simple blood-pressure test could detect an important warning sign. Taking preventative steps at this time could add years to your precious life.

- your weight: One of the major health problems in the United States today is obesity. It is reported that up to seventy percent of all people in our prosperous country are overweight. Generally speaking, when a person is overweight, it means that he or she is taking in more calories than the body requires for fuel. Too much weight adds stress to the physical frame and additional pressure on heart muscles, and it also makes it more difficult for the circulatory systems to function properly. (To give you some idea as to where you stand, take a look at the average weight table. And by the way, if you are under twenty-five and still in school or college, the issue of desirable weight norms should be covered in a health class.)

- other vital signs: In addition to temperature, pulse, blood pressure, and weight, your doctor will usually request a urine specimen to determine blood sugar levels and impurities that may result from a deficient filtering system. A thorough medical checkup should also include an examination of your eyes, teeth, ears, skeletal system, and other parts of your body where problems may be suspected.

After a thorough examination, your doctor will be in a better position to make some recommendations to help you take care of your health. There are a number of health guidelines that any person should follow to stay in top condition. Listen carefully to what your doctor recommends, and

Daily Calorie Needs for Men and Women

WOMEN

Age	Weight (Lbs.)	Height	Calorie Intake
10–12	77	4' 8"	2250
14–16	114	5' 2"	2400
18–22	128	5' 4"	2000
22–35	128	5' 4"	2000
35–55	128	5' 3"	1850
55–75	128	5' 1"	1700

(Pregnant women add 200 calories; nursing women add 1000.)

MEN

Age	Weight (Lbs.)	Height	Calorie Intake
10–12	77	4' 7"	2500
14–18	130	5' 7"	3000
18–22	147	5' 9"	2800
22–35	154	5' 9"	2800
35–55	154	5' 9"	2600
55–75	154	5' 7"	2400

---

keep those simple health suggestions in mind. Get plenty of sleep, based on your age, level of activity, and metabolism. Develop a regular program of exercise. If you are athletically inclined and are presently involved in some type of training program, you know the benefits that can be gained from physical fitness. However, many people are not in good physical condition, and they suffer from poor performance and lack of self-esteem. Consult with your doctor and get started on a sensible exercise program. Even after years of neglect and misuse, the human body has amazing resiliency and can be restored to good health in a relatively short period of time.

It is also important for you to try to eat well balanced meals. The body requires a certain amount of carbohydrates, fats, proteins, minerals, and vitamins—plus water—in order to function properly. If you have "tired blood' and often feel droopy, you may not be meeting your daily requirements of these five nutrients. (Take a look at the chart that lists basic calorie needs for men and women.) It is important to recognize that people in young adulthood require more calories daily than children or adults. Don't eat more than you need to! In most cases, with the proper amount of sleep, regular exercise, and well-balanced meals, you will feel better, look better, and have a more positive outlook for the future.

On a more personal note, I must point out that thousands, perhaps millions, of people's lives and careers have been ruined or cut short because of alcohol, tobacco, and drugs. The problems associated with these products have been the focus of world attention in recent years as never before in the history of civilization. I am certainly not an authority on the subject, but I could spend hours discussing actual cases with which I am familiar from personal experience where alcohol, tobacco, and drugs destroyed people's lives and families. I lost a dear uncle not long ago because of lung cancer. His hair came out and grew back three times from radiation treatments before he finally passed away. Regardless of the arguments about whether or not cigarette smoking causes lung cancer, I know that my uncle was a chain smoker.

There are some very important points concerning the danger of these products that I want you to keep in mind. People who manufacture, sell, and push alcohol, drugs, tobacco are in it for the money—they do not care about you or your future. Do not believe for one moment the myth portrayed on television that you need these things to be successful. Nothing could be further from the truth. The truth is that these things will keep you from success. You either break the habit or die before your time.

Do you remember the question that I discussed a while back? Who will you believe?

I hope that what I have had to say has helped you reevaluate your attitudes with regard to your health. Your health is the key to long-term success and happiness.

Desirable Weights
For Men and Women

Women		Men	
Height	Weight	Height	Weight
4' 10"	96–107	5' 2"	118–129
4' 11"	98–110	5' 3"	121–133
5' 0"	101–113	5' 4"	124–136
5' 1"	104–116	5' 5"	127–139
5' 2"	107–119	5' 6"	130–143
5' 3"	110–122	5' 7"	134–147
5' 4"	113–126	5' 8"	138–152
5' 5"	116–130	5' 9"	142–156
5' 6"	120–135	5' 10"	146–160
5' 7"	124–139	5' 11"	150–165
5' 8"	128–143	6' 0"	154–170
5' 9"	132–147	6' 1"	158–175
5' 10"	136–151	6' 2"	162–180
5' 11"	140–155	6' 3"	167–185
6' 0"	144–159	6' 4"	172–190

These weights are averages for people over age twenty-five. If you are a woman with a small frame, subtract six to eight pounds; with a large frame, add eight to ten pounds. If you are a man with a small frame, subtract eight to ten pounds; with a large frame, add ten to twelve pounds.

Good Health   83

Part Two: Review

I have read the four chapters dealing with the question "Where am I?"

☐ *I have a better understanding of where I am and know what I must do to become the person I want to become.*

☐ *I have a better understanding of my mind and how it functions. I know how to use my mind to achieve my short-range and long-range goals.*

☐ *I understand more fully that my greatest power is the power to choose and make the right decisions for my own life.*

☐ *I have a better understanding of the importance of my health and know what I must do to preserve and maintain it.*

If you cannot affirm each of these four statements by placing checks in the boxes, please go back and reread these chapters before proceeding.

FOOD FOR THOUGHT:

The Way to Happiness

Keep your heart free from hate, your mind free from worry. Live simply. Expect little. Give much. Fill your life with love. Scatter sunshine. Forget self and think of others. Do as you would be done to. Trust God. Thank God for all your blessings. Do all you can for people without thought of personal gain. Spread happiness.

Try this for a week and you will be surprised.

Part Three

Where Am I Going in Life?

"The potential for greatness lies within me, but success will come to me only if I make up my mind what I want!"

CHAPTER 8

The Prelude to Success: What Success Means to You

In our modern society, there is a word that has become very popular in recent years. People talk about it, authors write books about it, and everyone wants what it describes. I am sure you realize I am talking about the word *success*.

While working with our nation's public schools for the past two decades, I have had the opportunity to ask thousands of high school students a very simple question. "Would you like to be successful during your lifetime?" I can tell you truthfully that over ninety-nine percent of all students have answered yes to my question.

Now, what percentage of all adults in today's society would you consider to be successful? Would you say ten, twenty-five, fifty, seventy-five, or even ninety-nine percent? If your answer was less than ninety-nine percent, there is an issue you would do well to consider. What happens to the millions of people in the most economically prosperous nation in the world from the time they are idealistic and hold high expectations in school to the time in life when they reach the age of retirement? In short, do you think most people are as successful in life as adults as they thought they would be when they were still in school?

If you will give some constructive thought to what I am saying, I believe that you, too, will realize that part of the reason for the disparity between hopes and realities lies in the fact that most people never take time to define what success means to them. Because they never take time to define success and establish definite goals for their lives, they have no way of knowing if and when they have arrived. As a result, they just wander aimlessly through life.

At this point in your life, what does success mean to you? If you have not already done so, you must define what success will mean in your own life. To my way of thinking, this is one of the most critical points of the entire "How to PLAN YOUR LIFE" concept. It is the bridge that will move us from the abstract into reality, from just thinking about success to actually achieving it. Later on, when we talk about goal-setting, time management, communication, the free enterprise system, financial planning, and many other topics, the conclusions you reach at this point could serve as the cornerstone for your future. Do not miss what I am saying: it is almost impossible to achieve a lasting success unless you have first taken the time to define what *success* means to you.

I tried to explain early in the book that there are two distinct areas to consider when evaluating success: the person, and the job, career, or set of activities in which that person wants to be successful. I believe you will agree that success is much easier to understand when we break it down into these two areas.

Let's examine the realm of the person first. For the sake of example, let's say we are talking about you. What are some of the qualities you think you would need to be successful? Would it be important for you to be honest? Would you need to be fair in dealing with others? Would you have to act morally? Would you have to be dependable, loyal, trustworthy, and show a willingness to work? I could add many more qualities to this list. Which ones would you regard as most important?

When we combine these necessary qualities (which include many we haven't mentioned) we are really talking about your philosophy of life, your character, your integrity, and your value system.

Let's say you excel in all these qualities. Would this make you a success? The correct answer is "Not necessarily." You may be a fine person, but you are not a success unless you have applied these qualities to help you achieve something that you have decided to achieve. You must have a goal.

The second area concerns the job, career, or set of activities in which you want to be successful. You may as well face the fact that success in today's times requires money, at least in some minimal amount. Unless you have already achieved financial success, financial matters—including plans for financial security—will play an important role in your success.

From this angle, success rests on your greatest power—the freedom to make your own decisions. You are the one who chooses how you will spend or invest your time. For example, you might be willing to spend hours practicing a particular sport in order to be a professional athlete or win a gold medal in the Olympics. Of course, a number of factors enter into the picture, but your long-range goal is success, and the end result, or what you hope to achieve as a byproduct, is a lot of money. Isn't this true? Different people obviously will have different goals. One person might want to be a doctor, another to go into business, while still another might want a job in a factory. The end result of all jobs and careers, however, is to earn both satisfaction and money. The amount of money, whether large or small, is determined by several factors. What I want you to see at this point is that we need money to buy those things we need and want.

Would you be a success if you had a job or career or were in the process of preparing for a job or career in any one of fifty thousand possible occupations? Once again the answer is "Not necessarily." If you have a job and are working to pay your bills, but you have no commitment, no plans, no purpose, and no goals, then you are not a success. You become a success when you make up your mind what you want; decide the job, career, or activity in which you want to invest your time; determine how you will go about preparing yourself to earn the kind of income you desire; and develop a plan to achieve financial security.

My good friend Ethan Moore of Hattiesburg, Mississippi, gave me a definition of success that is better than anything I have ever heard on the subject. "That person is successful who finds what God intended for him to do with his life, prepares himself to do it, and does it daily to the best of his ability." I hope you are beginning to see that success is not so much a destination as it is a way of living. How are you going to live success?

Success has become more problematic since we became a highly mobilized, technologically advanced society. Parents and educators have long known the value of teaching the importance of good character, but have neglected the value of teaching students "success skills." Carefully considered decision-making and the development of short- and long-range goals would help students use talents and abilities to their maximum potential. The contemporary shortage of success training is particularly evident in the area of financial success, a fact underscored by statistics compiled by the Social Security Administration in Washington, D. C. Only five percent of all working people are financially independent at retirement age. This is after an average of forty years of opportunity in the most affluent society in the history of mankind. Financial success is not the only criteria for true and lasting success, but it is one measuring stick in determining the rate at which people are moving toward life goals.

If you want to achieve success in life, you must decide what success means to you and set some goals. Make each act of the day successful. This produces a successful day; a series of successful days produces a successful week; a series of successful weeks produces a successful month; a series of successful months produces a successful year; and a series of successful years produces a successful life. Just think, it all starts with one successful act.

Please answer the following questions to define what success means for you. To be a successful person, I need to possess the following qualities: _____
_____
_____
_____
_____

To give my life direction, purpose, and meaning, these are my specific goals: _____
_____
_____
_____
_____

FOOD FOR THOUGHT:

The Art of Success

There are no secrets of success. Success is doing the things you know you should do. Success is not doing the things you know you should not do.

Success is not limited to any one area of your life. It encompasses all facets of your relationships: as parent, wife or husband, citizen, friend, neighbor, and worker.

Success is discovering your best talents, skills, and abilities and applying them where they will make the most effective contribution to your fellow men and women. In the words of Longfellow, it is "doing what you do well, and doing well whatever you do."

Success is not confined to any one part of your personality but is related to the development of all the parts: body, mind, heart, and spirit. It is making the most of your total self.

Success is harnessing your heart to a task you love to do. It is falling in love with your work. It demands intense concentration on your chief aim in life. It is focusing the full power of all you are on what you have a burning desire to achieve.

Success is ninety-nine percent mental attitude. It calls for love, joy, optimism, confidence, serenity, poise, faith, courage, cheerfulness, imagination, initiative, tolerance, honesty, humility, patience, and enthusiasm.

Success is not arriving at the summit of a mountain as a final destination. It is a continuing upward spiral of progress. It is perpetual growth.

Success is having the courage to meet failure without being defeated. It is refusing to let present loss interfere with your long-range goal.

Success is accepting the challenge of the difficult. Listen to the inspiring words of Phillips Brooks: "Do not pray for tasks equal to your powers. Pray for powers equal to your tasks. Then the doing of your work shall be no miracle, but you shall be the miracle."

Success is relative and individual and personal. It is your answer to the problem of making your minutes, hours, days, weeks, months, and years add up to a great life.

Author Unknown

CHAPTER 9

Achieving Success by Meeting the Needs of Others

"Success is simple: it's not easy, but it's simple." Truer words were never spoken.

Have you ever stopped to consider that everything you want from life that you do not presently have is in the hands of others? If you will think about this a moment I believe you will realize it is true. If your need or desire is for more money, other people have it. If your need or desire is for a higher position in your job or career or in the greater arena of society, other people can give that authority to you. Should your needs or desires be more along the lines of psychological "income" and self-esteem, here again, other people can give this to you. I hope you will give this time to soak in, because it is a very important concept. Everything you need, want, or desire from life that you do not presently have is to be found in the possession of others.

At this time in your life, do you have needs, wants, or desires that are not being met? If your answer is yes, and these needs are to be found in the hands of others, how can you go about getting them? Will you take them, steal them, do without them, or earn them? If your answer is to earn them, congratulations—you are well on your way to a more suc-

"Sometimes when you are down, sad, or blue, it's hard to remember that you basically get back from others what you first give to them."

cessful life. If your answer is to do without them, you must recognize that your self-image and your subconscious mind are holding you back. Your fear of loss is greater than your desire for gain. If your answer is to take them or to steal them, you are not fully aware of some natural laws that operate in the universe. (I'll have more to say on this later in the book.)

Did you know that you can have almost anything you want if you are willing to earn it? If you know this, in all likelihood you also understand a natural law that controls everything in the universe. This law is known as the law of *cause and effect*, and simply stated, it claims that for every cause there must be an effect and that for every effect there must be a cause. It also means that good actions produce good results and that bad actions produce bad results. To state it in economic terms, it means that what we put out in service, we must get back in rewards. In the Bible it is stated still another way: "As you sow, so shall you reap." This law is inflexible like the law of gravity, so it works every time, whether or not we understand or know about it. This law allows you, as a thinking person, to tell your own fortune, because if you take care of the causes, the effects, without fail, will always take care of themselves.

At this point, I want to show how your needs, wants, and desires can be satisfied through an understanding of the law of cause and effect—with the result that you will become more successful. All human beings have needs, which at the most basic level encompass food, clothing, shelter, transportation, and medical care. We also have higher needs, including needs for love, approval, self-esteem, security, group membership, and self-actualization. In addition to our needs, most people in our affluent society have wants and desires. There is no limit to the things we could place on this list, but some of them might include luxury vacations, motor homes, golf carts, face lifts, and vacation cottages. To satisfy these needs, wants, and desires, it is necessary to earn or to have a great deal of money. As I tried to explain before, having a lot of money is only one form of success, but it is important to have enough to meet our needs in today's times.

As you think about the fact that everything you need, want, or desire that you do not presently have is in the possession of others, it is important to realize that other people have many of the same needs, wants, and desires as you. At the moment you begin to help other people get what they want, the law of cause and effect decrees that other people in turn will not only help you, they will make sure that you get what you want. Please remember that this is how the law of cause and effect works. The better the quality and quantity of the product or service you provide to others, the greater the rewards you will receive in return. Do not ever make the mistake of thinking this law does not work. Prisons, jails, halfway houses, and streets are filled with people who thought they could get something for nothing. Over the long haul, it just will not work.

The reason the majority of people in our society today are not successful is because they want maximum rewards for minimum effort or service. It is like the person who stands in front of a cold stove and says, "Give me heat, and then I will put in the wood." If you would like to achieve outstanding success, you must give more in value than you receive in return, especially in the beginning when you are developing momentum. You also must recognize that the rewards you seek will not always come directly from those you serve. The inflexibility of the law of cause and effect requires that the benefits will come, regardless of where from. Sooner or later, the scales will balance and you will receive everything you have earned. You will be happy because you will know down deep how you achieved it.

I want you to fix this natural law firmly in your mind. The only true and lasting success comes as a result of helping other people get what they want. Because of the law of cause and effect, the better the quality and quantity of the product or service you provide to others, the more rewards you will receive in return.

The law of cause and effect applies to every person. It is true that we are no better than the way we treat others, because these principles apply to one and all.

Man's Measurements

A man's no bigger than the way
He treats his fellow man!
This standard has his measure been
Since time itself began!
He's measured not by tithes or creed
High sounding though they be;
Nor by the gold that's put aside;
Nor by his sanctity!
He's measured not by social rank,
When character's the test;
Nor by his earthly pomp or show,
Displaying wealth possessed!
He's measured by his justice right,
His fairness at this play.
His squareness in all dealings made,
His honest, upright way.
These are his measure, ever near
To serve him when the can;
For man's no bigger than the way
He treats his fellow man.

—Author Unknown

FOOD FOR THOUGHT

According to the U.S. Department of Labor, over ninety percent of all job or career failures were due to poor attitude, inability to communicate effectively, or inability to get along with other people.

"In the race for life, I know I must make the effort to start before I can ever be a winner."

CHAPTER 10

Goals: How to Set Them and Reach Them

Ralph Waldo Emerson once said, "Every great and commanding moment in the annals of the world is the triumph of some enthusiasm." You may know that the word enthusiasm comes from the Greek *entheos*, meaning "full of God" or "inspired." I sincerely hope you are becoming enthusiastic about the ideas you are getting from this book and what they will mean to you and your future in the weeks, months, and years to come.

You will also need enthusiasm for another aspect of your path to success: goals. I have tried to make clear that you need to have goals to aim for and to challenge you to succeed. At this point, I want to get serious about explaining in layman's terms the importance of goals for your life and what action will be necessary to reach them. It may seem very elementary, but let's start by defining the word *goal*, so you will know exactly what I am referring to as we go along. A goal is any object or set of circumstances that one or more people would like to have or bring about. In short, goals are the things people want. These things can be tangible things we can see and touch or they can be intangible things we cannot see and touch. Although it seems like everyone should have a clear idea of what they want, the tragedy is that most people never clearly set any goal to achieve. Research has proven that only five percent of all working people in American have specific, written goals and can tell you what they are working toward at any given time.

I want to remind you of some things I have already discussed that have a tremendous bearing on the process of setting goals. The goals you have now and the goals you will set in the future are determined by your current self-image. This is why self-image has been called a life-governing mechanism. If your opinion of yourself and estimation of your worth is low, your goals will be low. If your opinion of self and your self-worth is high, your goals will be high. Does this make sense to you? Try to be realistic when setting goals for your life. Make your goals closely reflect your interests and abilities—what you reasonably think you can accomplish. You can increase the number and size of your goals over the coming months and years.

Another factor to consider is what you have stored in your subconscious mind. Your subconscious mind feeds you information that determines your self-image, but it is also the bank or reservoir of knowledge you must use to make your decisions, choices, and value judgements. If your subconscious mind is filled with mostly negative information, this will have a harmful and limiting influence on the size and nature of your goals. The converse is true if your subconscious is devoted to positive information: you will set realistic goals and be spurred on to reach them. You have to make your own decisions concerning goals you want to reach, but you cannot discount the background that your subconscious thoughts will provide for your decisions.

When it comes to setting and reaching goals in life, perhaps the most important concept is concentration. Remember the comment I made about how baseball players get the job done? How many fly balls can the right fielder catch at one time? The correct answer is one. During batting practice, before the game begins, a skilled fielder might be able to catch several fly balls one right after another, if they are not hit too far away from him. But the fielder can only catch one fly ball at a time during the game, because that is all he can concentrate on.

Like the baseball player who can only catch one fly ball at a time, you can only reach one large goal at a time. When you reach one goal, you can work toward another goal and reach it, then another, then another. But at any particular time, you must have at least one goal for yourself. Having goals to work for will add direction and purpose to your life. You should never wake up in the morning without a goal!

As you begin to consider specific goals for your life, things you would like to have or like to be, you should recognize the key qualities that your goals should feature. Your goals should be:

- realistic: Take your personal growth in sensible, logical steps and you will not get discouraged.
- attainable: How much money, time, and effort will this goal cost? Do you have the background, education, and experience needed to reach your goal at this point in time or will you need to acquire it in the future?
- written on paper: Written goals imply a commitment on your part. Each time you look at your written goals, they wil be driven deeper into your subconscious mind. Your mind will begin to function as a servomechanism.
- limited with respect to time: A time limit creates a sense of urgency and helps you avoid procrastination. A clear timetable for goal completion is a very important success habit.

- specified as either short or long term: Generally speaking, short-term goals are those that take less than a year to achieve. Long-term goals, which stretch over more than a year, allow more time for success but are more difficult to sustain.
- appropriate to all areas of your life: Keep your personal priorities in mind as you set goals and you will maintain a balanced life.

I have already asked you to set some goals for your own future success. At this point I'd like for you to look back to those goals (see Chapter 8) and transfer them to the format I have shown below. The process of transferring your goals and writing them down on paper will assist you in memorizing your goals, and they will become more clear with each repetition. In addition, specifying features of your goals, such as the projected completion dates, will make them more concrete and easier for you to reach.

Sample Personal Goals

Goal	Term	Date	Will goal require money?
New car	Short	July 1	yes
Courteousness	Short	today	no
Become president of company	Long	Dec. 1, 1995	yes
Savings account of $100,000	Long	Apr. 15, 1992	yes
Become a better spouse	Short	now	yes
Make the honor roll	Short	May 23, 1987	yes
Take public speaking course	Short	Sept. 1, 1987	yes

Goals	Term	Date	Will Goal Require Money?

Once you have your personal goals written on paper, with realistic time limits established, it will be time to begin to think seriously about how you are going to reach them. You should be able to see from the preceeding exercise that many of your goals will cost money to achieve. If you do not presently have the money you need to reach your goals, you will have to begin making the first steps to acquire those necessary resources.

I have tried to point out that the money you need to reach your tangible goals is in the hands of other people. In most cases, you will receive the money you need in return for the product or service you provide through your job or career or from investments you have made in the past. The more money you receive, the easier it will be to satisfy your needs and wants and achieve long-range financial security.

As you work to achieve success you must always keep your goals clearly in your mind, and revise them in light of your personal growth whenever that is necessary. After you have carefully outlined your goals, your work to achieve them will be the only mark of your success.

The Slight Edge:
It Only Takes Two Percent

Have you been working like a horse? I've been thinking about that expression—and at least one horse I can name has earned a pretty fair hourly rate.

Someone has figured out that the racehorse Nashua earned more than a million dollars in a total racing time that added up to less than one hour! That's pretty good pay. Of course, we know that many, many more hours went into preparing for that winning hour of racing.

But there is something else that interests me. What is there about a horse like Nashua that made him such a consistent winner and made him so valuable? You'd probably pay a hundred times as much for a horse like Nashua as you would for an ordinary racehorse. But is he a hundred times faster? No. To be a consistent winner and to be worth a hundred times as much as the average, he needed only to be consistent in finishing just ahead of the rest. All he had to do was win a good share of the time by a nose to be worth a hundred times as much as an also-ran.

And so it is with human beings who are on top in the game of life. A writer in a national magazine made the assertion that the difference between the man of achievement and the man of mediocrity is a difference of only about two percent in study, application, interest, attention, and effort. Only about two percent separates the winner from the loser!

A boxer can win the world's championship simply by winning one more round than his opponent—or even by being only a point or two ahead. And this narrow margin can make the difference between fame and fortune or never being heard of again. It's often a matter of only two percent.

We have no idea of what a change we could make in our results if we would simply add that two percent more time and effort than the average person is willing to put in. Do you think you're doing all you can? No one is doing his best who can do better. Just doing two percent better than your usual average job could improve your results a hundredfold!

It's something to think about.

GENE EMMETT CLARK

CHAPTER 11

Can Goals Be Too Big?

Before moving on to discuss specific ways you can reach the short- and long-term goals you have established for yourself, it is important that you consider an often perplexing question. "Can goals be too big?"

When it comes to setting goals for their lives, many people experience fear, concern, and even frustration because of what they think the consequences will be if they set goals that are too big. There is another reason that you might find interesting—many people do not set specific short- and long-range goals for religious reasons. Apparently, they believe that having faith in God to take care of them is all that is required. What these people fail to realize is that having the proper goals will help them develop and use the talents and abilities God gave them to their fullest potential. It's a matter of priorities.

When you wrote down your goals and tried to make them specific, you might have asked yourself some questions like these: "Can some of my goals be too big?" "Is it really possible for me to reach all the goals I have established for myself?" It is common knowledge that having doubts about yourself is just a part of life, and to some extent you just have to get

"It's better to shoot for a star and miss it than to shoot for a skunk and hit it."

accustomed to it. But when you let those doubts keep you from having the success and happiness you could earn if you went about it in the proper way, you are accepting the verdict while the jury is still out.

The question concerning the proper size of personal goals is perplexing for many people because the answer is both yes and no. For some people, maybe five percent of our nation's total population, the answer is yes. These are the kind of people who set goals that are so big they cannot possibly achieve them. Goal-setters of this type inevitably wind up totally frustrated. The problem for the other ninety-five percent of the population, however, is that they set goals that are too small or set no goals at all. These people (and the odds are good you fall in this group) almost never set goals that cannot be reached.

Remember, you are a very special, unique person. You can probably accomplish a lot more than you think you can. I have tried to explain that your greatest power is the power to choose, to make your own choices and decisions. While your choices and decisions may affect the lives of other people, in most cases, you will be the one who must live with the consequences. You need to make goals and commit yourself to reach them.

I think that we are protected from making goals that go too far. It is like you are born with an internal mechanism that tells you that you should not set a goal if it is not possible to achieve it. In my opinion there is good evidence for such a mechanism. Can you think of several things other people have achieved that you would never consider attempting? Because of this phenomena, chances are very good that you will achieve whatever you have set your mind and heart on.

Another great asset you possess is your latent untapped mental potential. Experts in the field of psychology point out that most human beings function using ten percent of their true mental potential. Since your mind controls your actions, reactions, your behavior, habits, attitudes, you should realize that developing and using more of your latent mental potential will make it possible for you to reach all or most of your goals.

An aspect of goals that you must pay careful attention to is consequences. When you begin to devise a plan to reach your goals, you should ask yourself, "If I am to reach this goal, what, if anything, will I have to give up?" We all have twenty-four hours each day and we must decide how and where we will spend or invest that time. If you have big goals and are in a hurry to reach them, you might have to take serious risks. To reach your goals, will you in the long run have to give up, lose, or perhaps harm your health? What about your family or friends? Your reputation? Could it ultimately harm your soul? Knowing the consequences, you must make the choice. At this point only you can determine your personal values and priorities. I think it makes sense to plan, determine priorities, take the time that is necessary, and enjoy the trip. Even taking the slower way I can still be a great success, financially secure and happy with myself. Usually, haste makes waste, and the stakes can be high!

When you look at your short- and long-term goals, you probably will notice they fall into three basic categories. Goals usually concern changes in *attitude*, advancement in *position or prestige*, or *accumulation of money*, for emergencies or retirement or to buy things that require money. Each type of goal has its own special requirements and time constraint. It is not always easy, but attitudes can be changed with the proper motivation and desire. It usually takes a lengthy time to acquire position or prestige, but if you set a clear goal and stick with it you can succeed. In most cases, the extra money you need and desire will come from increased performance and production from your job or career.

If you do have big goals, you should realize that you can reach only one goal at a time. Break those big goals down into a series of smaller, short-term goals that will provide encouragement and inspiration by successes that mark your progress. If this sounds simple, it's because it is simple—believe me, it works. "Inch by inch, anything is a cinch."

Can Goals Be Too Big? 111

Each new day brings a fresh, clean page for you to write the story of your life. Try as best you can to learn from your mistakes and failures of the past, and then forget them. Press on to the dreams in your heart.

Part Three: Review

I have carefully studied the material concerning the question "Where am I going in life?"

- ☐ *I have a clear understanding of what success means to me and the personal qualities that are necessary for me to achieve the success I desire.*
- ☐ *I understand more fully that the fulfillment of my presently unsatisfied wants, needs, and desires is to be found in the hands of others.*
- ☐ *I know the answer to the question "Can goals be too big?" and I am prepared to make and reach goals on my path to success.*

If you cannot affirm each of these three statements by checking the boxes, please go back and reread Part Three before proceeding.

FOOD FOR THOUGHT:

This is the beginning of a new day. God has given me this day to use as I will. This day is important because I am exchanging a day of my life for it. When tomorrow comes, this day will be gone forever, leaving in its place something I have traded for it. Therefore, I want it to be good and not evil, gain and not loss, success and not failure, in order that I shall not regret the price I have paid for it.

Heartstill Wilson

Part Four

How Will I Get There?

"Selecting the right job or career may not be easy for me, but I know the world will step aside if I know where I am going!"

CHAPTER 12

A Career or a Job?

You must decide how you wish to travel—by means of a career or a job. Let me explain what I mean.

I have asked you to define success and write your goals down on paper. Since many of your goals no doubt require money, money that you may not have at this time, you will have to earn this money by providing a product or service to other people. The vehicle or means you will use to earn this money will be either a career or a job. Since there is a vast difference between a career and a job in terms of potential benefits, I want you to see clearly what each involves. If you have not already chosen the route you will take, you must consider it carefully. It is a decision you really need to make wisely, because it will affect your life and your rewards for the rest of your productive days.

What is a job? In general terms, a job is usually a way to earn a living and pay the bills. It usually takes a minimum of training and education. In most cases, a job only requires that an individual commit to be on time, be at work almost every day, perform duties of the job satisfactorily, and relate and get along well with supervisory personnel and fellow workers. For the services rendered, the individual who performs the job is usually paid an hourly wage and additional fringe benefits such as vacation pay, sick leave, holidays, medical insurance, and workmen's and unemployment compensation. The idea of a good job sounds attractive to many people, and for some people it is a perfectly acceptable way of earning money. Quite often, however, the person who holds a job does not fully understand economic principles.

For example, if the job is in the private sector, the employee may not fully comprehend how this job relates to the profit motive of his employer. If economic conditions change and the employer begins to lose money, the employee with "job status" is usually the first to be let go. Of course, the person who loses a job can look for another, but if economic conditions are bad, jobs are scarce. This is one way that a job usually offers the individual less security than a career.

A career differs from a job in that it is usually seen as a long-term means of earning a living. It requires definite selection from the wide range of occupations that are open to consideration. The selection of a particular career is followed by a period of preparation, either in college and post-graduate school for such professions as medicine, law, engineering, and education, or in vocational-technical schools for trade careers. The armed services are also viewed by many individuals as good career choices, since the military provides education, training, and the opportunity for long-term service.

The person who opts for a career rather than a job usually earns a great deal more money because of more extensive education, specialized training, and a long-term commitment to stick with the chosen profession or career. It is the old story: in most cases you only get out what you first put in.

If you have a job and are not happy with the money you are earning or your prospects for the future, the solution to your problem may be a lot simpler than you realize. What many people apparently do not know is that a job can become a career almost overnight. All it requires is a change of attitude toward personal growth and a long-term commitment. The change in attitude for the jobholder might follow these lines: "I like the work I'm doing, and I'm beginning to see how the product (or service) I'm providing to other people is meeting their needs. I believe this line of work has a future, and I'm going to use the knowledge and experience I have as the foundation to begin to grow, to learn, and to serve." Friend, if you are thinking in these terms, you no longer have a job, you have a career. It's good to know that in general a career has a much brighter future than an ordinary job.

Consider the example of the person in a factory who goes to work for minimum wage on the assembly line. Let's say it's a bright young man who has initiative—soon he is promoted to foreman, then to department head, and finally to general manager. At some point in time, the paid employee's view of his daily activity has changed: what was once a job now is a career. Do you see what I mean? Can't you make this example apply to your own situation?

Of course you must like what you are doing if you want to make the change in attitude from job to career. Surveys reveal that seventy percent of all working people in America are unhappy in some way with their jobs. Many of these people could probably come to enjoy their work if they approached it with a positive attitude, but undoubtedly some people are simply not doing what they are best at.

I'd like to tell you something that is so simple you might not have thought about it: You will never be a great success and have true happiness in life if you are in work that you dislike or that you are totally unsuited for. You should ask yourself a series of questions about your work and work situation (if you are a student, you should already be looking ahead to the type of work you plan to enter in the future). Do I like my work? Do I like the people with whom I am working? Do I like where my work is located?

There are over fifty thousand possible vocations and careers from which to choose today. If you are happy in your career or job, you should begin to improve your performance and increase your income. This will in turn provide the foundation for a savings and investment plan for future financial security.

If you have not made your career choice or have an interest in making a change, you need first of all to do some planning. Start by outlining the fields of work in which you take an interest. Take into account your personal interests, likes and dislikes, aptitude, education, and previous experience. Think of the services or products that others need that you could provide. What are the fields in which you would consider entering a job or career?

_____
_____
_____
_____
_____
_____

Career selection is a very important decision for you. Before you make it, talk with others who are employed in the fields of work you are considering. What do these careers pay? What is the long-range potential? Would you be happy with the demands placed on you in these careers in terms of travel, hours per day or week, and work situations? You will spend a large part of your life carrying out your career decision, so consider your best alternatives and decide carefully.

FOOD FOR THOUGHT:

The world will step aside for the person who walks confidently on a well-planned path.

"When you base your actions on a true understanding of natural laws, it's like having an autopilot to steer you in the direction of your goals."

CHAPTER 13

Natural Laws and How They Affect Our Lives

You may have heard the old saying "I would rather be lucky than good any day." This motto might express a reasonable way to approach life and its many opportunities—so long as a person's luck holds out. What do you suppose happens when the streak of luck comes to an end? If you depend on luck alone, you are set up for trouble.

Your success and your future is much too important to leave to chance or luck. The key to moving beyond dependence on luck is a better understanding of natural laws and how they affect your life. It isn't really necessary at this point to theoretically elaborate or go into great detail about all of the natural laws that have been discovered. If you develop a clear understanding of basic laws, however, they can be used to your advantage in everyday life.

I am more interested in how well you do than I am in how much you know. You can be a brilliant person and still not achieve your goals. I believe I am safe in saying that the majority of unsuccessful people, those who continually experience more problems than they can handle, either do not fully understand natural laws and their effects or they do understand natural laws but go ahead and violate them anyway ("I can get away with it just this one time").

To begin, let's understand that there are two kinds of laws that affect our lives: man-made laws and natural laws.

Man-made laws are in the United States generated by what we call the democratic process. Citizens elect representatives to make laws that govern society. Not all man-made laws are necessarily good, but if a law is enacted through the democratic process in Congress, state legislature, quorum court, or city council the citizens who live under the legislative jurisdiction must either obey the law or accept the consequences if they are convicted of violating it.

Man-made laws are something we all know about, because we are confronted with them every day of our lives. If you have ever received a speeding ticket or been convicted of committing a criminal offense of any kind, you are even more aware of man-made laws.

There is a point that although obvious I would like for you to consider: you can break man-made laws time after time and never be caught. For example, you can drive your car much faster than the posted speed limit and never be apprehended—there are simply not enough law enforcement officers to catch all violators. Most people who obey laws do so out of respect for the law; others obey laws because they fear the penalty if they are apprehended and convicted of lawbreaking.

I have found that many people, especially young people, base their actions on the theory "It's okay to do it if you don't get caught." An attitude toward law based on this view might be successful for a while, perhaps even for a long period of time. Unfortunately, however, this view does not fully take natural laws into account.

A *natural law* is a sequence of events in nature or in human activities that has been observed to occur with unvarying uniformity. The key word in this dictionary definition is *un-*

varying. Given the same conditions, the law will work every time, whether or not you understand or know about it. A good example is the law of gravity, discovered by Sir Isaac Newton in the sixteenth century. If a little girl too young to understand the law of gravity walks off a tall building, which direction do you think she would go? If ten thousand young children were to do the same thing, which direction would they go? I am certain you know that the law of gravity states that they would all go down. The fate of each of the children in my example, in all likelihood, would be death. The outcome would not be affected by the fact that all or some of the children did not understand the law of gravity.

When it comes to your success and happiness in life, there are many natural laws that affect you each day, whether or not you understand them or know about them. Of course there are many natural laws that affect us in many different ways, but I am most interested in the laws that have the most bearing on personal success. There are two basic natural laws that will provide us with a solid foundation to understand and apply all other natural laws. These two laws are related to thought and action. These laws have direct influence on your success and happiness.

The Law of Thought: You become what you think about most of the time. What do you think about most of the time? Are most of your thoughts positive or negative? Do you look for new and better opportunities to serve other people?

The Law of Action: For every action there will be an equal and opposite reaction. As a result of your thinking, what actions do you take most often? Are they good or bad? Are your actions geared to serving others or do you expect something for nothing or maximum rewards for minimum effort?

I want to make a clear distinction between the terms *natural laws* and *success laws*. To avoid confusion I have avoided discussing success laws thus far. Recall the definition I stated previously: a natural law is a sequence of events in nature or human activities that has been observed to occur with unvarying uniformity. A success law, on the other hand, is the application of a natural law to a sequence of planned events in our daily activities that enable us to achieve success. In other words, success laws involve a complete understanding of natural laws and recognition that it is easier to work with them than it is to work against them. How many people do you know who waste their time and energy and become frustrated because they continually violate the natural laws of the universe? (Of the many books that have been written on success laws, two I have in my personal library are *Laws of Success* by Napoleon Hill and *The Laws of Success* by Sterling W. Sill. If you want to know more about employing natural laws to foster daily success, you might begin with these books.)

I have developed a partial list of some of the natural laws and success laws that could benefit you. While the explanations I offer are a good start, you should gradually become more familiar with them. Don't hesitate to research them further—you will be enhancing your growth to success!

Important Natural Laws and Success Laws

The Law of Abundance: An entire forest can spring from a single acorn, and the contributions you make will be returned to you fantastically multiplied. Nature and human personality are equally rich—you only have to develop and use the potentialities that lie in them.

The Law of Advantage: One small well-placed jack can lift a heavy truck. Human beings can use a wide variety of mechanical, social, mental, and personality tools that multiply and magnify natural strength.

The Law of Appreciation: Giving honest and sincere appreciation to others is one of the best and easiest ways of gaining power. The law of appreciation is paradoxical, however: you should not expect others to give you honor in return for the appreciation you give them.

The Law of Chance: Over an extended period of time, good breaks and bad breaks will average out. We live in a world of law and order, not one of chance. We should be diligent in following the laws of nature, for they are ordained for our benefit.

The Law of Compensation: There is an appropriate compensation for every act. No one can do a good deed without receiving a reward at some time, in some way; conversely, no one can do something evil without suffering some penalty. (This law is also known as the Law of Consequences.)

The Law of Concentration: When a person concentrates all available energies on one specific task, the possibility of success is greatly increased. When time and talents are divided among several enterprises, chances of success are proportionally reduced.

The Law of Conditioned Response: You are capable of directing your appetites, ambitions, and all of your personal resources in specific ways to accomplish particular objectives. The key is the development of success habits, which will make right decisions and actions easier as time goes by. (For a deeper understanding of this law, take a look at the experiments in response conditioning of the scientist Pavlov.)

The Law of Courage: Courage is the quality of mind that meets danger or opposition with firmness. Isolated performances of great deeds do not make individuals heroes or cowards, they simply reveal character to the eyes of others. Every successful life needs challenges, hurdles to overcome, and problems to solve in order to bring the power of courage into play.

The Law of Diminishing Returns: Beyond a certain point, the addition or increase of economic production factors such as capital and labor will yield proportionally lower increases in total production. There is a point at which additional investment of resources is not worth the gain it will produce.

The Law of Dogmatic Statement: A rigidly formed dogmatic statement usually arouses hostile and negative reactions, but a properly qualified, well-considered claim usually elicits positive response and a more uninhibited transfer of ideas. Dogmatic statements can be even more divisive if the speaker is inconsiderate of the feelings of the listeners.

The Law of Example: One of the greatest forces in the world is the power of example. Example is how human beings learn morals, manners, and most essential knowledge.

The Law of Experience: Only human beings have the ability to record their experiences. This capacity has provided a unique heritage for our enrichment and practical benefit. By surveying and examining past experience, we are able to recognize clearly and accept the good, as well as to identify and avoid the bad.

The Law of Fear: Fear is not a curse, but is rather a great and constructive force. It can be life-saving if we are afraid of the right thing at the right time.

The Law of Fusion: The whole is judged by the part—and the part is equally judged by the whole. One tiny spot of rot in an otherwise healthy apple requires that we classify the apple as diseased, and recognize that it endangers other apples nearby. A practical application of this law is the fact that environment has a great influence on individual growth. We are judged by the company we keep.

The Law of Goals: Success becomes much easier when you have a strong commitment to a goal or objective that is clearly visualized and greatly desired. It has been said that "genius is the power to visualize the objective."

The Law of Growth: Growth is always a process of struggle. Those who do not persist in the struggle fail to grow, and are marked for premature elimination. You can coast if you want—but the only direction you will go is downhill!

The Law of Health: Most mental problems—and consequently most physical diseases—begin with inertia, lack of planning, idleness, and the habit of running from problems.

The Law of Hypochondria: A hypochondriac is a person that is habitually subject to imaginary ailments. Hypochondria emphasizes complaint and self-centeredness and is a dangerous barrier to the life of success.

The Law of Idleness: The inevitable result of idleness—with regard to physical, mental, spiritual, social, or personal development—is weakness. Inactivity is for this reason virtually equivalent to self-annihilation.

The Law of Instincts: Unlike all of the lower creatures, which spend their lives directed and controlled solely by instincts, human beings have the additional capacities of thought and reason. Instincts nevertheless serve an important function in human life. An important part of education is to recognize, understand, and cultivate these powerful and valuable inner tendencies.

The Law of Love: Love is a complex emotion of affection or regard that impels one to appreciate, take pleasure in, and delight in others. Love is devotion and attachment; it is magic. If you have love in your heart, before long it will be on your face, in your eyes, in your footstep, and in your handshake.

The Law of Loyalty: Loyalty means constancy and faithfulness in any relationship, and it implies trust and confidence. To implement loyalty successfully, we must think thoughts of faithfulness and then put them into action. Loyalty is not a gift that is simply given; it is a superb accomplishment.

The Law of Maturity: When you become an adult, you should act in a mature, responsible way in every area of your life. Knowledge alone is never enough to prevent confusion and failure. It is effective only in concert with the wisdom that comes from experience.

The Law of Motion: A body in motion—that is, in the act or process of change of position—tends to remain in motion until acted upon by some outside force.

The Law of Natural Selection: In biological conflicts, the fittest test specimens will be the most likely to survive. Individual variations advantageous to an organism in a certain environment tend to become perpetuated in later generations.

The Law of Probability: Since it is possible to measure the effects of given causes in most every circumstance, it is also possible—if all of the relevant facts are known—to predict results in advance. By being able to forecast future events, you are able to intercede in your own behalf to improve your chances for success.

The Law of Reason: Reason is the quality of sense and understanding that is the guiding and directing faculty of the mind. Cultivation of reason is a necessary condition for true success. One of the most important ways that the rational capacities of logic and judgement can be developed is by being conscious of poor judgement and faulty logic as it is manifested in both yourself and others.

The Law of Relativity: All of the manifestations of nature are fundamentally united. Discussion of this law most commonly refers to the principle of the interdependence of matter, energy, space, and time formulated by Albert Einstein.

The Law of Self-Pity: Self-pity is a feeling of real or imagined unworthiness, an inferiority complex that abandons hope, an allergic reaction to self. Self-pity is often born out of paying too much attention to the things that one lacks rather than being grateful for what one does have.

The Law of Self-Preservation: Self-preservation is often referred to as the first law of nature. Human beings have an inborn instinct that causes them to act in a manner that prevents their own destruction.

The Law of Symbols: A symbol is something that stands for something else: it is an emblem, type, or character. Symbols grow with tradition, and in time the acceptance of a symbol becomes a confession of faith. The interesting fact about symbols is that power and prestige associated with a symbol is somehow transferred to individuals who proclaim allegiance to it.

The Law of Teaching: One of mankind's greatest discoveries is that understanding can be communicated, excellence can be taught, and faith can be encouraged. No matter what your occupation, you should have a clear understanding of the learning process and a commitment to pursue education for the rest of your life.

The Law of Vision: Vision is the ability to project plans and hopes beyond the boundary of present circumstances. The person who has vision thinks about and prepares for the future, while the person who lacks vision lives only for the present.

The Law of Will: The power of conscious deliberate action is what we refer to as will. It is the faculty by which the rational mind makes choices regarding the ends of actions and directs the energies necessary for carrying out its determinations. If you seek success and happiness, you must learn to think. But you must also learn to make your thoughts and feelings subject to your will.

The Law of Words: Automobiles run and airplanes fly, but human beings literally talk themselves forward. A mediocre idea well expressed is often more effective than a better idea that is poorly expressed. Words are the most powerful success tools available to human beings.

You are a very special and unique person. I know you have a desire to learn the right things and the good things that will help you reach the goals you have set for yourself. Why do you suppose that some people live by the theory that there is never enough time to do anything right, but there is always time to do it over?

If you have a clear understanding of the laws of nature and can see their relevance to your quest for success, you are on the road to a great future.

FOOD FOR THOUGHT:

"A mind is a terrible thing to waste."

-motto of the
United Negro College Fund

"It's when the going gets tough that the tough get going. You can do it!"

CHAPTER 14

The Demands of True and Long-Lasting Success

Unlike many of the other chapters in this book, which I begin with a statement, quotation, or thought-provoking idea, I want to begin this chapter with a warning.

> **Warning**
>
> What I am going to say here appears to be so simple and obvious that you could pass it over and never realize how close you came to the truth. If you pay close attention, what I am going to say could give your life meaning, direction, and purpose, and in the process could help you achieve everything you have set your mind and heart on during your lifetime.

At this point, I am going to assume that you completely understand that your self-image and your subconscious mind affect everything you think about and everything you do. You should have your goals written down on paper, divided appropriately into categories short and long term. You should realize that in most cases the additional money you need to reach your tangible goals will come from your job or career, and you either should have that job or career now, or if you are in school or college, you should be in the process of making the necessary decisions for your future career. You also should be becoming more aware of how natural laws affect your life day after day.

If we continue this logical sequence of thoughts and ideas we naturally come to two important issues: how to secure the best job or career and how to make the most of it. First, in the event you do not already have the job or career position that is right for you, how do you go about getting it? When the basic education is complete, what steps lead to a satisfying profession? Second, once you have that job or career, what attitudes, habits, skills, and actions will be required for you to become a great financial success, at least to the point that you will be able to meet your needs and achieve your financial goals? Let's take these two questions in order.

There are a number of steps you should take in order to secure the job or career position that is right for you. Many experts agree that the foundation is a well-prepared *resume*. Develop a neatly typed resume that outlines your relevant personal characteristics, education, and previous employment experience. Be sure to include references and a statement explaining why you would be an asset to your potential employer.

Compile a *strategy list* of potential employers you would like to have interview you either in private or public sectors. Use this list as a guide for researching the companies or agencies for which you might be working. Plan your interviews with the information from your strategy list as a basis.

Everyone knows, of course, that the *interview* is the bottom line. Take special care to dress appropriately; do not dress too casually or too formally. Be conscious of your personal hygiene—make sure that your nails, hair, and face are clean. Try to look your best. Smile, and let yourself relax.

See the person who interviews you not as the personnel director or manager, but as a "purchasing agent." The person doing the hiring is going to make a purchase on the open market. Based on the law of supply and demand, that personnel director is going to make the best purchase possible for the company or organization. When you stop to realize that it may cost up to one hundred thousand dollars to train an entry-level employee for a specific job or career, you begin to see what is at stake. A personnel director has to be careful when making employment decisions!

In simple terms, you must be able to sell a potential employer on the fact that you will prove to be worth more than it costs to recruit and train you. It is obvious that the employer also expects a return on the investment. While you are a very special and unique person, an employer will see you in terms of profit or loss—and a potential loss is not a viable job or career candidate.

I am certain that you know that once you have the job or career that is right for you, you will have to work hard to make it a success. What are the attitudes, habits, skills, and actions that will be required to become a great financial success?

My view is that the best way to start on the road to success is by having a service attitude. The overriding feeling that a serving person projects to the consumer is one that says, "You are important, and I understand that my job or career is in existence to meet your needs. Without you—you who buy or pay for my product or service—it would not be necessary for me to be here." Surveys reveal that success is eighty-five percent attitude, and only fifteen percent knowledge and skill. You must develop a service attitude and foster that spirit while working with customers and clients.

Good value for the one who pays for your product or service is absolutely necessary for success. Millions of people in our country are held back from earning more money and achieving greater success because they do not fully understand this concept. The real boss in the competitive free enterprise system is the consumer. People and organizations produce products and services and offer them for sale, but economically speaking, nothing happens until they are sold to the consumer. When two or more people or organizations offer the same product or service for sale, this gives the consumer a choice. In most cases, the consumer will spend money only in such a way as to receive the greatest value.

Here is how this concept applies to you: make certain that your product or service is worth more to consumers in value than they are asked to pay for it in money. How do you feel when a restaurant raises the price of a hamburger and cuts down on the meat?

A motivational expert was asked, "What is the best way to become a success?" He replied, "*Hard work!*" The other person then eagerly asked, "Okay, what's the next best way?" In recent times, technology has changed the way we work. Machines perform many of the functions that were once done by hand, but the person who becomes an outstanding success today is still the one who knows the value of hard work.

There is an important difference, however, between working hard and working both hard and intelligently. I want to say that successful people are the ones who work hard and intelligently. That means that unsuccessful people either are lazy, dishonest, or expect something for nothing or they work hard and are honest, but have never been taught self-management skills and the steps to achieve success. Hard work is irreplaceable, but it must be directed by intelligence and training.

There are basically three groups of people in the world: Those who make things happen, those who watch things happen, and those who wake up later and wonder what happened. Which group are you in?

Persistence is the one personal quality you can control above all others. Only you can determine when you will quit. When the going gets tough in a job or career, the first impulse of most people is to throw in the towel, to quit.

The Chinese have a proverb: "If you will live with a disaster for three years, it will turn into a blessing." Give yourself a chance to succeed. Focus on a service attitude, value, and hard work. Don't give up if something doesn't work the first time. Give the challenge time to turn into a blessing.

You must work hard, improve your skills in what you do, and believe in yourself to increase your value. As you do this, your income will also begin to increase. The more money you earn, the easier it will be to manage it and achieve financial security.

Whether you are self-employed or employed by someone else, you must begin to acquire self-management skills. You must manage yourself before you will be qualified to manage others. How well do you manage your time? Your money? Other resources? To truly be a valuable employee, you must put management to work to make the most of the resources available to you.

Press On

Nothing in the world can take the place of persistence. Talent will not; nothing is more common than unsuccessful people with talent. Genius will not; unrewarded genius is almost proverbial. Education will not; the world is full of educated derelicts. Persistence and determination alone are omnipotent.

Part Four: Review

I have read the material dealing with the question "How will I get there?"

☐ *I understand the difference between a career and a job. If I do not have the career or job that is right for me,*

based on my interests, aptitude, and skills, I am taking the steps necessary to secure that position.
☐ *I have a better understanding of natural laws and how they can be used to help me achieve personal success.*
☐ *I understand the personal qualities that I will need to be successful in my career or job on a day-to-day basis.*

If you cannot affirm each of these statements by placing checks in the boxes, please go back and reread these chapters before proceeding.

FOOD FOR THOUGHT:

Don't Quit

When things go wrong—as they sometimes will—
When the road you're trudging seems all uphill,
When the funds are low and the debts are high,
And you want to smile but you have to sigh:
Rest if you must, but don't you quit.
Life is queer with its twists and turns
As every one of us some time learns;
And many a failure turns about
When he might have won had he stuck it out.
Don't give up though the pace seems slow—
You may succeed with another blow.
Success is a failure turned inside out
The silver tint of the clouds no doubt.
And you are near when success seems far,
So stick to the fight when you're hardest hit—
It's when things seem worse that you mustn't quit!

Author Unknown

Part Five

What Kind of Person Will I Be?

"My values, morals, and beliefs become fixed as I grow older. I am therefore, going to take special care to make sure that they work for me and not against me."

CHAPTER 15

Self-Examination: Values, Priorities, and Rewards

I hope you are excited about the new and beautiful things that are going to happen in your life as you set in motion the goals and plans you have established for yourself. As you think about the concepts we have explored in previous chapters—your self-image, the power of your mind, goal-setting, natural laws, and job or career success strategies—you should be prepared to get serious about putting your plans into action.

I want you to picture yourself standing on top of a hill, ready to go down the other side. I am sure you know that going downhill is a lot easier than going uphill. That is exactly where you are now! Look at it this way: it is going to take just so many days to reach your goals. Since your days are going to be made up of many different types of activities, both on and off your job or career, I believe it is important to be successful in several areas of life—the areas I think are most important. Success is only complete if it involves success in the four major areas of life: spiritual growth, the family, your job or career, and income. In fact, I think it is a good idea to identify for each of your written goals which area it relates to most closely.

Are you beginning to get a sense of how simple success really is? Once you make up your mind what you want and set your goals, success becomes a matter of doing certain things in certain ways until you achieve those goals. It is just as easy as writing things on a want list and checking them off.

It is important that you periodically pause and examine your values, your priorities, and the rewards most important to you. You might wonder why such a self-examination is necessary. You do know what happens when an automobile tire goes flat, don't you? The tire will not roll true even after it is repaired until it is balanced once again.

What I mean, of course, is that you can be a tremendous success in one or more of the areas of life yet still be unhappy—if your life is out of balance. Many apparently successful people are frustrated and unhappy, and they never understand why. Simply stated, their lives are out of balance. My purpose in saying this is not to try to tell you how to live your life or what you should believe or think. How you arrange your life is your own private affair and responsibility. As an American citizen, you have personal freedoms and individual rights guaranteed by law, and I would be willing to fight and die to defend those rights.

After many years of work in the field of human resources and personal development, I have become convinced that many people fail to take advantage of their opportunities because they never were taught or they never learned what their real choices were. For example, let's say you were given a multiple-choice question like this one.

To be successful in life, it is necessary to

    a. get on welfare.
    b. inherit money from relatives.
    c. take a job and steal from the employer.
    d. know the right people.
    e. marry a person who is rich.

Which choice would you make? You probably realize that all of these choices are wrong, but unfortunately millions of people go through life restricted to a closed set of poor choices. Because of environment or mental conditioning (remember what I said about "garbage in, garbage out"?) they fail to understand that there are other choices that could result in tremendous success.

    f. get a good academic or vocational education.

    g. be worth more to your employer that you are paid.

    h. develop a service attitude toward the customer.

    i. save ten percent of your income to invest later.

    j. stay with the same job or career long enough to build momentum and achieve success—don't quit!

    k. base your life on complete and total honesty.

Webster's Dictionary defines the word *value* as "that which is desirable or worthy of esteem for its own sake; a thing or quality that has intrinsic or inherent worth." To state it more simply, when something has value, it is not necessary to take from it or add to it; it is worth interest in and of itself.

We value things in life that are both tangible and intangible. Things we value of a tangible nature might include our homes, cars, land, money, business establishments, and other material possessions. Things we value of an intangible nature might include love of family, friends, and country, or career, personal freedom, and life itself. Since valuation is a personal matter, different people find different things to be worthy.

We also value certain attitudes and forms of human behavior. These values translate into actions, feelings, thoughts, speech, and eventually in day-to-day ways of life. We judge others in light of our own personal values, but society also establishes values to which it expects its members to conform. I believe the greatest problems we have in the world today are created by people who have different values but must interact with one another in some aspect of business or social life. A value system is the code a person lives by. Each one of us has personal and moral values and also is influenced by social values, traditional values, and religious values.

Moral values are those relating to the distinction between right and wrong. Each of us is born with a moral conscience that tells us what is right and what is wrong. (This is not to be confused with knowledge, which comes into the "empty box" of the mind through the five senses.) Every society, however, determines the standards that are acceptable for its members; moral standards therefore vary from place to place. For example, what is morally accepted in San Francisco, California, might not be morally accepted in Montgomery, Alabama. You are penalized by society if you violate moral laws while you are living, and you will be judged for your actions by an Almighty God when you die. You might violate the laws of man for a while, but there are greater laws that cannot be broken without paying a price.

In addition to establishing moral standards for itself, society also establishes other values. Examples of *social values* are the work ethic, respect for the property and rights of others, a commitment to the quality of life, and a unified goal of national defense. It is important to notice, however, that social values are generally held in a loose fashion, with the result that different individuals might find them more or less compelling.

There are *traditional values* that have been handed down from one generation to the next, that can be traced back to the beginning days of our nation's existence. These include marriage, the family, and church. Most of the traditional values in our country are derived from a spiritual heritage based on the Bible. For this reason, traditional values are closely tied to *religious values*, which also play an important role in American history. The Constitution of the United States guarantees separation of church and state, but history reveals that our early forefathers placed great emphasis on religious beliefs and religious values. In a general sense, your personal values are the sum total or composite of all the moral values, social values, traditional values, and religious values that mold and shape your life. Have you thought about where your personal values come from?

Who has had the most influence on your values at this point in time?

_____ parents or guardians   _____ friends
_____ teachers in school   _____ relatives
_____ neighbors   _____ religious leaders
_____ co-workers   _____ television personalities

Are the people who have influenced your values as happy and successful as you would like to be? _____ yes _____ no

As you consider your future success, happiness, and financial security, and based on your present understanding of natural, man-made, and moral laws, would you, under any circumstances commit any of these actions?

Yes	No	
_____	_____	lying
_____	_____	stealing
_____	_____	cheating
_____	_____	dishonesty
_____	_____	giving less than your best to the one who pays your salary

Do you remember the law of cause and effect?
_____ yes   _____ no

The next matter of importance is *priorities*. Your priorities are those things in life that are most important to you. To clarify your personal priorities, rank the success areas listed below in order of their importance in your life.

    _____ family
    _____ job or career
    _____ income or money
    _____ spiritual life

Regardless of what you say, a pretty good indication of your priorities is how you spend your time and money. Do you agree?

Of course, to make a thorough self-examination you must know what *rewards* you will seek to obtain in your quest for success. If you recall, a reward is a desired goal or end result of your job, career, or any labor or effort that you expend to complete a task. Rewards include a wide range of tangible and intangible things, from the money you receive in exchange for work to the personal satisfaction of a challenge met or achievement well done.

You alone can determine the rewards that will have the greatest importance for your own life. Will you focus on amassing a fortune in money, or perhaps on saving enough to guarantee financial security? Will you seek the life of pleasure that material possessions offer? Will you try to develop a position of prestige in your company or community, and enjoy the recognition and respect that fame brings? Or will you emphasize personal relationships, stressing family ties and close companionship with those who think the way you do? Will you devote your life to loving others? Will you try to make all of your actions service to God? Do you hope for the happiness and fortune of good health? Or is your aim the security of inner peace, the feeling of calm that pervades even difficult situations?

Of course, there are many rewards that you can seek in your life. What is important is that you carefully consider what you want your life to accomplish, and that you devote yourself fully to accomplishing that objective. Consider the rewards you will seek carefully—what you aim for will determine the direction of your life!

FOOD FOR THOUGHT:

"Really and truly, what kind of person am I?"

"Our forefathers had the wisdom to separate church and state, but faith in God is the cornerstone of our nation."

CHAPTER 16

Spiritual Life: An Often Untapped Power

If there was a source of power available but unknown to you that would help you have a real purpose in life and achieve true success and happiness, would you like to know about it? If you are a thinking, compassionate person, chances are good that you already know about the power I have in mind. As I have explained before, I respect your right to think and believe as you choose. At the same time, I cannot in good conscience write a book about life-planning and never mention your spiritual life.

There is a source of power available to you that you may or may not be using, and it is the greatest bargain in the world—it is free! Come to think about it, it is one of the few things in today's world that is free. I am referring to the unlimited source of power that comes from an Almighty God when we strive to be in the center of his will.

Since recorded history began some six thousand years ago, the peoples of the earth have sought to find favor with their gods. There is a created spirit within each of us that reveals something bigger than we are. Even pagans know this, for every civilization and culture has devised ways to honor and worship this higher power, whatever their conception of that power happened to be. The concept of a supernatural or almighty God varies somewhat, depending on the culture. For example, some Eastern cultures view God as somewhat impersonal, and others often have the idea that there are many gods. But many centuries ago, the concept evolved in Western culture that there was but one all-knowing, all-present, all-powerful God.

The yearning for religious freedom played a great part in the settlement and development of our country. In the sixteenth and seventeenth centuries, many of our forefathers left their homes in Europe to settle here in America. Many countries were represented, but in England the Church of England, which functioned as state church, had dominated people's religious lives. Because of this, when our forefathers drafted and later adopted the United States Constitution, it contained specific provisions to separate church and state. The separation was not devised because they wanted to keep God out, but because they sought to prevent history from repeating itself with government or state once again dominating the religious lives of citizens.

During the long, hard winters of the early years of our nation's history, many of our Puritan forefathers placed great faith and hope in an Almighty God. Reference is made to Divine Providence in the Declaration of Independence, passages of scripture are carved in stone on buildings in our nation's capitol, and our currency bears the inscription, "In God We Trust." This influence continues to the present day. For example, President Ronald Reagan declared 1983 the Year of the Bible. It would be difficult to deny our nation has a spiritual heritage.

To be sure, the United States of America has undergone many social and economic changes in recent years. There are people in America today who seek to remove God—and all other forms of spiritual emphasis—from our society. Because we are constituted with the ability to think, reason, and exercise conscious will, our climate of freedom allows that we choose what we will believe and how we shall live.

It might be of interest for you to know, however, that the individuals who have grown up in America in homes where religious training was stressed have generally not run into trouble with the law. Recent studies have shown that less than five percent of those convicted of crimes come from Jewish homes, fifteen percent from Catholic homes, and thirty percent from Protestant homes. The vast majority of those convicted of crimes have had no religious training at all. Based on this fact, why do you suppose some people would like to take God out of our social and political life?

While your spiritual life is a very personal and private thing, it, like all other areas of knowledge, comes back to a question I posed early in this book: "Who will you believe?" You can find millions of people in America today who believe in God as a source of power for life; on the other hand you can find thousands of others who do not believe in God. It really comes down to you, doesn't it? Who will you believe?

Some time ago, I received a little book, *Power for Living*, that was printed and distributed free by the Arthur S. DeMoss Foundation. In this book a number of noted people give personal testimonies concerning what God means to them in their lives. Some of the people who share their stories are Roger Staubach, former quarterback of the Dallas Cowboys; Wallace Johnson, co-founder of Holiday Inns; N.B.A. basketball star Julius "Dr. J." Erving; Chuck Colson, former counsel to the President of the United States; and Olympic ice skating champion Janet Lynn. These individuals, like millions of others, have found that God is always present in times of trouble, need, and personal distress. I personally do not know how people survive in today's times without God as part of their lives.

Who can consider the gift of life itself, look at a beautiful sunset, wonder at the flowers that bloom each spring, or see a wild deer grazing in a meadow and not feel the presence of God? For me, the reality of God is not a matter to debate, it is a matter to appreciate. I may not know what tomorrow holds, but I know who holds tomorrow. Your spiritual life is simply too important to neglect. What good is material success if in the process of acquiring it you miss the whole point of life?

It is a good idea to recognize what area of life each of your goals concerns. Look back at your list of goals (Chapter 10) and transfer to the spaces below those that deal with spiritual growth.

_____
_____
_____
_____
_____

FOOD FOR THOUGHT:

A Wall of Prayer

Build a wall of prayer around that home
And those you love;
Take them to the Father
Who sees and hears above.
List each thing that's dear to you;
Record it where it stands—
Be careful now to put it all
In the Father's hands.

Build a wall of prayer around
That journey that you make—
When riding in your car
Let God the steering take.
Don't trust to luck or driving skill,
Ask Him to be there;
Build for yourself and those you love
A mighty wall of prayer.

Build a wall of prayer around the place
You worship in;
'Twill help to keep it free
From greed and hate and sin.
Build a wall of prayer around the one
Who speaks for Him;
That those who come to listen
Will turn away from sin.

Build a wall of prayer around
Just everything you do—
As you seek Him day by day,
He will see you through.
Life will be more glorious
Every single hour,
As He reveals His love to you
Through His wondrous power.

Glenn E. Wagoner

"Truth, honesty, hard work, and moral character are not ou of date; these virtues are just as important today as they wer two hundred years ago."

CHAPTER 17

The Role of the Traditional American Family

Many authorities agree that the traditional American family is important to our nation's future. Yet in recent years we have seen a tremendous assault on the traditional family. The reasons are quite complex, but the results for individuals and the nation as a whole could be devastating.

Before we can clearly understand the problems facing the family, we must first develop a basis of information about the family. Let's examine the history of the traditional American family. What is the family, and how is it composed? Why is it important? How has it contributed to our nation's success? What is its importance for the future?

First, what is a family? Dictionaries give a number of definitions, but most of them closely relate to one of three basic senses: a group consisting of two parents and their children; a group of people related by blood or marriage, that is, relatives; or a number of people descended from a common ancestor, in the sense of tribe, clan, or race.

Almost from the beginning of recorded history, people have lived together in family units or shared common households. However, the traditional American family came about as a result of a religious concept of marriage. In this view, the family is formed by the marriage association of one man to one woman, and it includes as well the children born as a result of the marriage union. The traditional American family arose in the climate of the spiritual heritage of early colonists who sought the free exercise of religion. Those colonists, who were our forefathers, believed in God and read and obeyed the teachings of the Holy Bible. The concept of marriage—one man to one woman—was therefore the foundation for the home or family unit, and children born into the home expanded the family circle.

In the early days of our nation's history, the family was important for two basic reasons: economic necessity and mutual defense. Economic times were so hard that family members had to stick together and work together just to survive. The dangers of pioneer life also required that family members cooperate in protecting one another. Families later banded together in what came to be known as settlements as a way to provide protection from wild animals and hostile Indians.

As you probably know, the family today has experienced many changes from the early days of family life in America. Some changes have been responsible for the breakdown of family values, which has issued in increasing divorce rates, a decline in ethical and moral character, and increasing crime. It has become such a national problem that a White House Conference on Families was held to explore ways to strengthen the American family and the traditional values it fosters.

Many of the trends in our society that have contributed to the breakdown of family values arise from economic and job-related factors. Economic pressures brought on by inflation have made it necessary for many families to have two incomes. Working women now comprise over fifty percent of the labor force. In addition, the nature of work in this country has changed with the move from an agricultural to an industrial to an informational society. "Farmer to laborer to clerk" might serve as a brief history of the American economy. Since it is much easier (not to mention more appealing) to process information than to work in a coal mine or a steel mill, it is no surprise that more women now work outside the home. With the increase of working women, the women's rights movement has de-emphasized the traditional role that a woman takes in the home as wife and mother. Apart from the question of how it has affected the status of women in society at large, it has affected the family. One example of this is in the field of the religious and moral training of children, which is traditionally done in the home. When loving mothers of young children are not in the home to provide this training, society reaps the consequences.

"Show me the homes of a nation and I will show you what kind of nation you have." That is a statement worth thinking about, for it points out how the family's strength reflects on the strength of social relations in general. Let me show you what I mean.

The Meanest Mother in the World

As a child, I had the meanest mother in the world. She was really mean. When other kids ate candy for breakfast, she made me eat cereal, eggs, and toast. When other kids had cola and candy for lunch, I had to eat a sandwich. As you can guess, my dinner, too, was different from other kids'.

My mother insisted on knowing where we were at all times. You'd have thought we were on a chain gang. She had to know who our friends were and what we were doing. She insisted that if we said we'd be gone for an hour that we be gone for one hour or less. She was really mean.

I am ashamed to admit it, but she actually had the nerve to break the child labor laws. She made us work! We had to wash the dishes, make all the beds, learn to cook, and suffer all sorts of cruel things. I believe she lay awake nights thinking up mean things for us to do.

She always insisted on us telling the truth the whole truth and nothing but the truth. By the time we were teenagers she was much wiser, and our life became even more unbearable.

None of this tooting the car horn for us to go running out on dates. She embarrassed us to no end by making our dates come to the front door to get us. I forgot to mention that while my friends were dating at the mature ages of twelve or thirteen my old-fashioned mother refused to let me date until I was fifteen or sixteen. She was mean!

My mother was a complete failure as a mother. None of us has ever been arrested or beaten by a mate. Each of my brothers served his time in the service of his country—and served it willingly, no protesting.

And whom do we have to blame for this terrible way we turned out? You're right—our mean mother!

Look at all the things we missed. We never got to take part in riots, never burned draft cards, never got to do a million and one things our friends did.

Our mean mother made us grow up into God-fearing, educated, honest adults. Using this as a background, I am trying to raise my children. I stand a little taller and I am filled with pride when my children call me mean.

The Role of the Family 159

You see, I thank God He gave me the meanest mother in the world!

Author Unknown

We each have families to some degree. You have two parents who are the result of a genetic pool that goes back thousands of years. You might have brothers and sisters, aunts, uncles, and cousins. You might be married, single, divorced or widowed.

The importance you place on family and how family values fit into your future plans depends solely on you. If you are a mature, responsible person, you must make the choice for yourself where family fits into your success and happiness. I personally believe it is important that we, the citizens of America, place a renewed emphasis on family values and the family tradition. The greatest resource in this country, in my opinion, is young people. The leadership skills, values, and commitment to high ideals that we instill in them by example—within the context of family—will determine the quality of life in our country for generations to come.

It is important that you identify which goals you have set that concern family relations or values (look back to Chapter 10 for your original list). As you think about family goals, you should bear in mind that many marriages fail because husbands and wives do not set goals that are compatible, or because they do not set them together with a mutual commitment to achieve them.

_____

_____

_____

_____

FOOD FOR THOUGHT:

Children Learn What They Live

If a child lives with criticism,
He learns to condemn.
If a child lives with hostility,
He learns to fight.
If a child lives with ridicule,
He learns to be shy.
If a child lives with shame,
He learns to feel guilty.

If a child lives with tolerance,
He learns to be patient.
If a child lives with encouragement,
He learns confidence.
If a child lives with praise,
He learns to appreciate.
If a child lives with fairness,
He learns justice.
If a child lives with security,
He learns to have faith.
If a child lives with approval,
He learns to like himself.
If a child lives with acceptance and friendship,
He learns to find love in the world.

CHAPTER 18

The American Free Enterprise System

It has been said that most people think they want more money than they really need, but they settle for a lot less than they could earn if they went about it in the right way. In today's times, we all need a certain amount of money to function as responsible members of society. The comparative amount of money you will desire depends on your needs, lifestyle, and obligations, past, present, and future.

The problem I see in the cases of many people is that they earn a sufficient amount of money but lack the self-discipline and management skills to take care of their money once they earn it. Financial security therefore depends very much on income and investment plans. But even more fundamental for your success is a basic understanding of the free market economic system. While it is possible to earn a lot of money without understanding the system, it is even more possible to succeed if you work in the system in a knowledgeable way. For example, knowing how the free enterprise system works should provide some insights as to what to do when economic conditions change and your career or job plans require reevaluation.

"I know I must put in the coal first, before the heat will come out. And I know I must serve the customer or the one who pays my salary before I can earn the money I need and desire."

What is the American system? What do we mean when we talk about free enterprise or a free market policy? I think there are two central features, the first of which is a specific political system. In this country, the system of government recognizes the power of the individual citizen. We call this system democracy, the rule of the majority. Provisions in the United States Constitution guarantee that individual citizens have rights to life, liberty, and the pursuit of happiness. It is important to see that these foundational rights implicitly include the right to own property, raw materials, and production facilities. This right of ownership is not recognized under other political systems, such as dictatorships or socialist regimes, in which the individual citizen has very few rights and the government or state owns the land, raw materials, and production facilities.

The second important aspect of the free market position is its role as an economic system. When private citizens use their land, raw materials, and production facilities to produce products and services in excess of what they need for survival, a surplus is created. This surplus is sold to consumers to meet their needs. The area in which this activity takes place is called the *market place*. The term *free enterprise* simply means the freedom that private citizens have to produce products and services and sell them to consumers for a profit. It is the free flow of products and services, without undue government interference, that makes this system so unique. The free market is in fact so unique that with only six percent of the world's population and seven percent of the world's land mass, the United States produces over twenty-five percent of all the manufactured goods in the world.

What does this mean for you? As an American citizen, you are one of the most fortunate individuals on the face of the earth. You have the right and the opportunity to find a place in this system—anywhere you choose. When you apply your knowledge, skills, or special training to meet the needs of consumers, you are in a position to earn profits or help your employer earn profits. You are free to keep a portion of these profits for yourself to do with as you please. In short, the reason our economic system is so great is that individual citizens have the incentive to get ahead. We can all be winners if we just know how to go about it.

The free market is divided into two distinct sectors based upon ownership. The public sector includes service agencies and organizations in which all of the land, buildings, and other resources are owned by the general public. These resources are managed and controlled by the various levels of government in our country: federal, state, district, county, and municipal. Citizens elect public officials to manage and supervise public resources and provide services that private individuals cannot provide for themselves, such as national defense, highway maintenance, health care, mass transportation, utilities, and various human services. To provide these services and so fulfil the needs of citizens, the various levels of government must hire vast numbers of employees to coordinate and run the public agencies. These employees are called "public employees" whether they work for the federal, state, district, county, or municipal government. (This group also includes all the individuals employed by our nation's public schools and colleges.)

A job or career in the public sector is desirable for a number of reasons. Some people are attracted by the opportunity of public service. A public job also has the appeal of security, since it theoretically will be in existence for many years to come. An occupation in the public sector commonly offers generous fringe benefits, including retirement, insurance, paid vacations, sick leave, and an opportunity for advancement. Public jobs and careers also feature pay scales with built-in raises based on length of service, qualifications, and increased responsibility.

In case you did not know, all public employees—including those individuals elected to public office—are paid from revenues generated by taxes of one form or another. In general, all members of society pay taxes; those with larger incomes pay more, but even those individuals who have little or no income pay some taxes in the form of sales taxes, gasoline taxes, and other tax surcharges. There are over fourteen million public employees in our country today. All of them must be paid from revenues generated by taxes or loans made by the government.

While public service jobs and careers offer a great place of service for many people not presently in the system, the fact that salaries for these positions depends on stable tax revenues is a matter to consider. Many experts think that the trend in the next two or three decades will be to reduce public employment because of the tremendous national debt (over two trillion dollars). There is a reason for this, and it is important for you to understand. When the number of public employees becomes so great that the tax burden on the private sector diminishes the incentive to produce, a stagnant, sluggish economy results. Layoffs begin in both the public and private sectors, the unemployment rate rises, and other problems in the economy begin to crop up. The key to a healthy economy, therefore, is balance between the public and private sectors. You cannot have more people riding a wagon than you have pulling it without suffering serious consequences.

The *private sector* is the area of open market economy in which free enterprise takes place. While the government does have the power to regulate the private sector and tax business, industry, and individuals to support itself, its stance towards business is theoretically "hands off." Businesses in the private sector are owned by one or more private citizens. The oldest type of business ownership, which is perhaps the most traditional, is the *single proprietorship*, in which one individual owns and runs the business. In *partnership* two or more individuals share ownership. A relatively modern innovation in ownership is the *corporation*, a legal entity that is supported by shareholders who purchase stock. In the *closed corpora-*

tion stock is held by family members or a closed group. On the other hand, stock in a *public corporation* is available to the general public and usually can be purchased through the stock market.

The purpose of every business in America, regardless of its type of ownership, is to produce products and services to meet the needs of consumers. The price for a particular product or service and the quantity sold depend on a number of factors, but ultimately they are subject to the law of supply and demand. If the demand is high and the supply is low, the price will be high; if the demand is low and the supply is high, the price will be low. In today's times, the law of supply and demand must be understood in terms of a global economy, with the boundaries of the marketplace stretching far beyond national borders. Supply and demand is also affected when the government subsidizes a particular product or industry or uses products for political purposes.

The element that protects the consumer in our free enterprise system is competition. One business or company cannot charge too much for a particular product if there are others who produce the same product and sell it at lower cost. Consumers will spend their money where they think they can get the best deals, valuations which may or may not be based on price alone. (Japanese imports have had great success because consumers rated them as good deals.) Quality service and product perception may also influence consumer choices.

The most important aspect of the American free enterprise system is *profit*. Profits are determined by taking the difference between the selling price of products or services and the total cost of production. Any excess of income after production costs are paid is the profit that sustains a business. Profits provide salaries for management and labor, and facilitate the paying of fringe benefits such as retirement, insurance, vacation, and sick leave. Profits pay returns on the investments of those who have run the risk of putting up money to start or run the business—the owners or shareholders. The company that is successful in generating profits can expand its production or sales capacity, and thereby provide more jobs for the community. As we have noted, profits also sustain the public sector, contributing to the tax base to support public services.

How can you best take advantage of the opportunities that the free enterprise system provides? If you are currently employed in the public sector or have a desire for public service, first understand that taxpayers pay (or will pay) your salary. Develop a plan to upgrade your skills and job qualifications, in order to serve the best you can in your position. Set your sights on the job level and income you desire and stick with your plans. In time you will reach your goals. Remember that financial security is determined not so much by how much you earn as by what you do with your salary.

If you are employed or wish to be employed in the private sector, understand that in this realm the consumer is the real boss. Your rewards will be determined by how well you serve the consumer. You or your employer must earn a profit to provide the money you need for the future. Develop your creativity. Look for new and better ways to provide the products and services your customers need and want, and then deliver on your ideas.

Regardless of what part of the economic system you find a place in, always be tuned to the bottom line. Who is paying the bill? When you know the answer to this question, you will be in a much better position to control your future.

Job or career goals play an important role in your success in general. Look back at the goals you have set (Chapter 10) and transfer your job or career goals to the spaces below. Feel free to add additional goals as you desire. (As usual, be sure your goals are specific and have set time limits!)

_____

_____

_____

_____

FOOD FOR THOUGHT:

The Customer

The customer is the most important person in our business.

The customer is not dependent on us—we are dependent on him.

The customer is not an interruption of our work—he is the purpose of it.

The customer does us a favor when he calls; we do not do him a favor by serving him.

The customer is a part of our business—not an outsider.

The customer is not someone to argue or match wits with.

The customer is a person who brings us his wants; it is our job to supply those wants.

The customer deserves of the most courteous and attentive treatment we can give him.

The customer is the person who makes it possible to pay our salaries.

The customer is the life-blood of this and every other business.

CHAPTER 19

Income for Present Need and Future Security

Wise old Benjamin Franklin once said, "The secret to wealth, if you desire it, is to augment your means or diminish your wants. Either will do but you will acquire wealth faster if you will do both at the same time."

It is important for you to have a basic understanding of *income*: what it is, where it comes from, and some of the factors that will determine your income goals. As I have stated before, there are two forms of income. Tangible income is the class of those things we receive for services or goods in a form that we can see and touch. The most obvious form of tangible income is money. Intangible income includes all the things we receive as payment but cannot see or touch. Inner satisfaction, happiness, pride of ownership, and self-esteem are a few manifestations of intangible income. While intangible rewards are necessary for a healthy self-image, they do not directly affect your financial security (you cannot use intangible income to pay your monthly bills!).

Let's concentrate for now on tangible income. There are many forms of tangible income, but money is the only one that is completely negotiable—money can be traded for anything, at any time, in any place (at least in any country

"The only people who *make* money work in mints. The rest of us must earn it by providing products and services that are helpful and useful to others."

that accepts your currency). So let's talk about money, and discuss how you can earn, save, invest, and possess all the money you need and desire. To gain deeper insights into the subject of money, there is a series of important questions.

What is money? Money is in its most basic sense a form of wealth. In your mind, travel with me back to the earliest days of our nation's history. When the first boatload of settlers came to our shores, they saw land, water, timber, and wildlife. Settlers later discovered petroleum, minerals, and other naturally occurring resources. In the beginning, these natural resources constituted the standard of wealth. As early settlers began to convert these natural resources to meet their needs— land to produce food, timber and other resources to build homes, wool and animal skins to make clothing, and wood, metals, and animal bones to produce tools—these items gained in value and became components of wealth. As individuals became more proficient at their skills and crafts, and specialized in making or producing certain things, they began to trade items back and forth. Although this system, called *barter*, was initially useful, it eventually grew in complexity and unwieldiness. Soon it became necessary to have some medium of exchange so that trading would be easier and more convenient.

Money was thus introduced as a medium of exchange. A person worked to produce his specialty and either sold it for money or traded it for something of value to him. If he received money for his product he could use the money to buy the supplies that he needed. If the value of the products or commodities involved in a trade were not of equal value, the party who received the greater value gave the other party "something to boot"—originally an extra traded item, but more and more as time passed a sum of money.

We see from the early history of money that money is not pure wealth, it just represents wealth. It is only a medium of exchange.

Where does money come from? Money in one form or another has been used by every civilization since the beginning of recorded history. In the United States, the Constitution (Article I, Section 8) gives Congress the power to "coin money, regulate the value thereof, and of foreign coin, and fix the standards of weights and measures." Congress therefore has the authority to coin and print money. In its earlier days, the United States was on what is called the *gold standard*—coins and currency represented a particular amount of precious metal redeemable from government reserves. Various denominations of gold coins were minted (perhaps you have seen or owned a twenty-dollar gold piece) along with copper and silver coins. Printed or paper money in various denominations was originally backed by reserves of gold and silver. The gold standard was abandoned later, when the total value of printed currency exceeded federal reserves. The government adopted the present Federal Reserve Note, which is simply an official government I.O.U.

What determines the value of money? In today's economy, the price of a particular product may vary from vendor to vendor. For example, a particular suit might cost one hundred dollars at one store, but the same suit might sell for one hundred fifty dollars at another store. On the other hand, a twenty-dollar bill represents twenty dollars of purchasing power regardless of where it is spent or invested. This is where the customer is king, because the customer chooses where the money will be spent. To explain this, let me return again to our historical past. In the beginning, when money was first coined, let's say we had one plow produced and one twenty-dollar gold coin minted. What is the value of the twenty-dollar gold coin? I believe you can see it is one plow, because that is all that is available for purchase. If you extend this same principle and multiply it billions and billions of times, you will have the same thing that applies today. The value of our money is determined by the quantity and quality of all the goods and services available to purchase. It is in this sense that money is purchasing power.

Congress established a series of Federal banks to oversee the printing and distribution of our currency, free and independent of political pressures. That series of institutions is called the Federal Reserve System. The Federal Reserve System determines the amount of money printed and released in our economy. This is regulated by the amount of interest charged to banks who borrow from the government. The final aim of the Federal Reserve System is to serve the needs of society by contributing to economic stability.

You no doubt have been affected by inflation. We all have. Most people think inflation is just high prices. It does lead to that, but it is not the cause of inflation.

Inflation occurs when more money is released than the total value of products and services produced in a given accounting period. At that point we have too many dollars chasing too few goods. Inflation hurts every American, especially elderly people, who are living on fixed incomes, and the young and uneducated, whose earnings are low. These people have problems purchasing life's basic necessities in inflationary times. Any person contributes to inflation who does work of poor quality or produces less in value than the amount paid as salary or wage. Our economic system is very complex. You may wish to take economics courses or do additional reading in books that go into more detail. For example, there are several economic terms that I think you would do well to look up in a dictionary or economics text book: *GNP* (gross national product), *balance of trade, stock market, grain futures, unemployment rate, national debt, world bank,* and *consumer price index.*

The average American is becoming more involved in the decision-making process in matters that affect daily life. In practical terms, this means that we are moving from a representative form of government to a participatory form of government. How can I go about earning more money? You might in time change your basic decisions concerning how and where you live and the job or career in which you choose to spend your life, but the way you earn more money will remain basically the same. The reason I explained inflation and its causes is because you can earn more money each year, but if the inflation rate is higher than the percentage of increase in your earnings, you will have less purchasing power. (I remember the days of the five-cent Coca-Cola!) There are many ways to have more money—sound investments, speculation, gambling, theft, and fraud are possible candidates—but the best way to guarantee that you will have more money is to earn it by providing products and services to others that are needed and useful. I want you to consider your present or future job or career in light of these five qualities. I think that you will see that they are great opportunities for earning more money.

Find a need and fill it. For a job or career to be secure, there must be a real and permanent need for your product or service. Examples of permanent needs are clothing, housing, transportation, recreation, and entertainment. Products or services that provide for these fundamental needs have a good start at success. On the other hand, jobs and careers based on fads, get-rich-quick schemes, and seasonal activities are subject to rapid and often unsettling changes.

Duplicate your product or service. This is the principle used by chain stores such as McDonald's, Wendy's, Kroger, Sears, or Penneys. Another example is the manufacture of a particular product, such as Levi's jeans. In this case, the move is from one pattern to millions of copies—duplicate pairs of Levi's jeans. The principle is duplication, which saves both money and time.

Develop something unique. Make the consumer want to use your product or service more than those of your competitors. If you succeed, they will spend their money with you or your employer.

Earn a profit. Whether you are self-employed or employed by others, your extra money will come from profits. Lack of profits means no raises, and eventually it means a failed business.

Manage your money. You can earn more money, but if you do not manage it wisely, you will not achieve financial security. Remember that the steps to financial security—earn, manage, save, and invest—must all be taken for success in money matters to be complete.

What are your money goals? How much money do you want to earn each year for the next three years from salary, commissions, dividends, and other forms of income?

        19_____ : $_____
        19_____ : $_____
        19_____ : $_____

When I earn more money what should I do with it to have peace of mind and achieve financial security? One of the most basic steps to financial security is to provide life, health, disability, and funeral insurance protection for your loved ones. Term life insurance is pure protection and can protect a person in the early to middle earning years at very reasonable rates.

It's important to develop a personal budget. The battle of income vs. outgo is not easy to win, but a budget will help you see where your money is going each month. List income and expenses and review it at the first of each month.

Carefully examine your credit policy. How much of your monthly expenses are going for credit purchases? Can you pay these off without adding more? How much interest expense do you have each month in different fields: home, auto, furniture, recreation equipment, and so on? Are you paying more interest each month than you are earning in a savings account? If you are, it could be a sign of trouble.

The wise answer to the credit problem is to establish a regular savings plan. The primary reason most people are not financially secure is because they never develop a savings habit. Think of your credit purchases a moment. Do you really like the people at Sears, Exxon, and the bank more than you like yourself and your family? Then why not pay yourself each month, too? How much money can you save each month? Can you save more a year from now? Two years from now?

My Savings Plan

Year	Monthly Savings Goals
19___	$ _____
19___	$ _____
19___	$ _____

With your saved money, you will be able to develop an investment program. People who are not in the habit of saving usually do not have an investment program. They do not have the money to invest. It takes time, work, and self-discipline, but you can do it, if you have not done so already. Save five to ten thousand dollars and get started. People who have money have learned to make money work for them. Earning from five percent to ten percent interest on a savings account will help offset inflation, but the person who buys a hundred acres of land for six hundred dollars per acre, subdivides it, and sells off one-half acre lots for fifteen hundred dollars each will earn much more. If the real-estate investor is in a position to owner finance, he can earn additional income from the interest payments received. This is just one example of investing. There are many ways to invest: the stock market, futures market, mutual funds, stocks, bonds, new businesses, or existing businesses.

The person who invests money is expecting that money to grow; the rate of growth usually depends on the risk factor. As a general rule, if the risk of losing the money is high, the return on the investment will also be high. Conversely, if the risk is low, and the investment is relatively safe, the return will be much lower. While this equation does not always hold true because of the number of factors involved, it is a useful rule of thumb. You can't go to second base and keep one foot on first base—you have to decide if the risk is worth it.

The final reason for handling money wisely is because, at one point or another, you will no longer be working for a living. I believe you should determine the amount of money you will need each month for retirement income whether or not you plan to retire. This income can come from any source, but it should be set aside for this specific purpose. (Of course, you need to make a will for your retirement years—as well as for the present—that will distribute the proceeds of your estate without excessive legal fees or probate costs.) What about *your* retirement?

My Retirement Plan

When I reach my sixty-fifth birthday, I should have a guaranteed monthly income of $_____ per month for the balance of my life.

Part Five: Review

I have read the chapters dealing with the question "What kind of person will I be?"

☐ *I have a clear understanding of my values and my personal priorities, and a good idea of the kind of rewards I want from life.*

☐ *I think often about my relationship to God, and recognize that spiritual life is a vast source of power.*

☐ *I understand more fully why the traditional American family is important to our nation's future. I see clearly* the choice I can make or have made concerning the role I will play in it.

☐ *I have a better understanding of the American free enterprise system, including the public and private sectors, and I know how I can best use the economic opportunities our system provides.*

☐ *I have a plan to earn more money and savings and investment goals to insure some measure of financial security at retirement time. I have thought about this whether or not I plan to retire.*

If you cannot affirm these five statements by marking the boxes, please go back and reread Part Five before proceeding.

Part Six

What Must I Do to Make Success Happen?

"I do have a lot of time when I think about my entire life. But how much value do I get from my time every day? Do I use every hour?"

CHAPTER 20

Managing and Using Time

As you begin each new day of your life, what is the one thing you have in common with every other living person? The correct answer is that you have exactly the same amount of time each day: twenty-four hours—no more, no less.

You have undoubtedly heard someone say, "I can't do that because I don't have time." That is an untrue statement. What that person really means is, "I won't do that because it is not important enough for me to use, invest, or waste my time." Most of us say things like this because we do not wish to hurt other people's feelings. However, how you ultimately use, invest, or waste your time is determined by your priorities—what is most important to you. Do you agree?

In this chapter, I want to explore the subject of time and how to manage it wisely to achieve success. The average life expectancy in the United States is approximately seventy-five years. Some people live much longer, while others do not live as long. From a practical standpoint, you have no way of knowing just how long you will live, unless you have been diagnosed as having a terminal illness. However, you do know your birth date (_____), the point

_{Month   Day   Year}

when your life began. Barring unforeseen circumstances, you should have a pretty good idea how much time you have remaining to accomplish your goals and do some of the things you really want to do. When you begin to view time in this light, it becomes a very valuable resource, doesn't it?

The Structure of Time

60 seconds per minute X 60 minutes per hour
 = 3,600 seconds per hour

60 minutes per hour X 24 hours per day
 = 1,440 minutes per day

24 hours per day X 7 days per week
 = 168 hours per week

The key fact to remember is that you have 168 hours each week of your life!

If you want to use your time wisely as you seek success, you must understand that time is money. In the past, when life was slower and most families produced their own food, clothing, shelter, and other necessities, time was not viewed in the same context as money. Today, however, when we purchase over ninety percent of our needs from others, time is money. The fact that our economy is based more on services than on goods is most evident when we hire someone to perform a service for us. For example, we must pay the plumber who fixes the faucet for the time he invests so that he can pay others to perform services for him that he has no time to do himself.

The actual value of your time is determined by the size of your goals and your commitment to them. If you have big goals in which you have invested substantial commitment, that signifies that your time is very valuable on a unit basis. On the other hand, weak commitment to small goals means that time is not so valuable.

The person without goals could be compared to the old bum kicking a tin can, saying, "Here's to the holidays, all three hundred sixty-five of them." However, bums have to eat, too. Remember that proper use of time depends on goals and commitment.

For the greatest profit, time should be divided between productive time, rest time, and discretionary time. *Productive time* is time spent preparing for thinking about, planning, and actually working on jobs or careers. With all the emphasis these days on leisure, many people have lost sight of the fact that most rewards in life come from work. The important question with regard to productive time is the dollar value that you earn by investing it. How much is each hour of your productive time worth? To determine this, divide your total earnings or salary by the number of hours you worked. For example, let's say your gross earnings total $50,000 per year. If your average time spent on a job is 10 hours per day, that means 50 hours per week or 2,600 hours per year. The gross income divided by hours worked yields a time value of $20 per hour. Of course, your actual productive time will vary depending on vacations, sick leave, holidays, and so on.

My Production Goal

My financial goal—the total amount of money I want to earn this year—is
$_____. To reach this goal, I will need to earn an average of
$_____ per hour of productive time.

Rest or sleeping time is important from a value standpoint too. If you are not happy with the way you feel most of the time, you might consider the quality of bedding upon which you are sleeping. Human beings usually spend over one-fourth of their lives in bed. A good night's rest will usually improve your disposition and performance.

Discretionary time, the time when we are neither producing or sleeping, generally involves rewards that are not directly material. It is usually left to you how you will spend or invest your discretionary time. If you have done a good job of managing your time and have sufficient money to meet your needs, you can feel relaxed about leisure. You haven't really succeeded unless you can enjoy the time you spend alone or with family, friends, hobbies, recreation, church work, and other volunteer or service activities.

He Hadn't Time

He hadn't time to pen a note,
He hadn't time to cast a vote,
He hadn't time to sing a song,
He hadn't time to right a wrong,
He hadn't time to love or give,
He hadn't time to really live.
From now on, he'll have time on end,
He died today, my "busy" friend.

In today's society, we see many people who have ruined their lives and their health by becoming workaholics. In the early years of a person's job or career, it may be necessary to work long and hard, but with age, experience, and self-management skills, you should be in a position to enjoy the fruits of your labor. We can burn the candle at both ends, and it does produce a brilliant flame, but it sure is hard on the candle!

My Weekly Time Budget

How do I spend my time?

    Productive time   _____ hours per week.
    Sleeping or rest time   _____ hours per week.
    Discretionary time   _____ hours per week.
    Total   168 hours.

Suggested balance:

    Productive time   50 hours per week.
    Sleeping or rest time   56 hours per week.
    Discretionary time   62 hours per week.
    Total   168 hours per week.

Consider this information from a recent study on time management. The average American over eighteen spends his or her time during the 168 hours available each week as follows:

Sleeping	53.0 hours
Working	26.0 hours
Eating	8.0 hours
Watching television	43.0 hours
Listening to radio	17.0 hours
Reading newspapers	4.2 hours
Reading magazines	3.3 hours
Listening to tapes and records	1.3 hours
Attending movies, sports, and cultural events	0.3 hours
Reading books	0.2 hours
Other activities	11.5 hours

Why not keep a record for one week and see where all your time went? The point of finding out how you use your time to reach your goals is to allocate time for specific tasks every day. If you remember, I said that the value of your time is determined by the size of your goals and your commitment to them. For the past several years I have used a very special idea to help me manage my time each day. This time-management concept, often referred to as the $25,000 idea, has appeared often in various books and self-improvement articles. This idea will only help you achieve greater success and earn more money if you will apply it to the most important goal you are working to achieve. Remember, no goal means no success.

First write down on paper the six most important things you have to do the following day. You may want to do this late in the evening or early in the morning. Go over the list and number the items in order of their importance. Be sure each item on the list will move you toward your major goal.

As you begin your day, put the list in your pocket or purse and begin working on the first item. Stay with this task until it is complete. If something should force its delay, go on to the next item on your list. This way, you will always be working on the most important things in order of their importance. If you cannot finish tasks with this method, you probably could not finish them with any other method—or you would take ten times as long.

Make up a fresh list each working day. If there are items left over from the day before, simply put them back on your list in order of their importance. This will take all the confusion out of your work and your life. Follow these steps and you will never find yourself wondering what you should do next. The real issue that confronts you is whether you are strong enough to stick to your plans and reach your goals or weak enough to permit distractions to get you off course. Be careful to guard your productive time. If you choose to permit others to distract you from work during productive time, use your discretionary time to make up the work that you missed.

Hesitation

On plains of hesitation lie the bones of those who chose to die by standing still. They refused to take a side, or when accused of fault or wrong would not defend their convictions to the end. Their thinking was not positive. They had no arguments to give. By inaction they paid the cost, for "He who hesitates is lost."

Julien C. Hyer

"I now realize that if I'm not careful, I won't have habits, habits will have me!"

CHAPTER 21

The Force of Personal Habits

Have you ever heard the expression *the moment of truth*? Well, that is where we are in this book. No plan, no goal, no dream you have is worth a dime if you do not intend to carry it out or achieve it. Alan Bellamy, a good friend of mine who owns a chain of grocery stores, explained it to me one day: "We don't pay on potential, we pay only on performance." The moment of truth is that time in any person's life when the planning is over, the stage is set, the cheers of the crowd have died down, and the time to perform has come.

In your heart, you know whether or not you are serious about your plans, your goals, and your future. Your subconscious mind and your self-image will have a great deal to do with whether or not you are willing to make the effort, but in the final analysis, you and you alone must write the final chapter of your life story.

Human beings are creatures of habit; we get in the habit of thinking in certain ways and acting in certain ways. If we have good habits, they work for us. If we have bad habits, they work against us. It is that simple.

What is a habit? A habit is some action performed over and over again until it is done without conscious thought.

Brushing teeth each morning is a habit for most people. We also get in the habit of acting and reacting in certain ways to life's challenges.

How are habits formed? Habits are formed in one of two ways: from conscious action or subconscious action. Habits formed from conscious action are developed when you deliberately think of an action and then perform it while it is fresh in your mind. Psychologists have concluded that it takes twenty-one days of conscious action to form a desired habit. Think of the desired habit each new day and repeat it. Repeat it again and again, and after twenty-one days, it will have become a habit. You will no longer need to consciously think about it. However, if you miss one day of that twenty-one day period, you will have to begin all over again and go twenty-one more days before your new habit is formed.

In contrast to conscious habits, habits formed from subconscious action are in most cases those that cause the greatest problems. If your subconscious mind is mostly filled with positive information, the odds are good that your subconscious mind will produce success habits. On the other hand, if your subconscious mind is mostly filled with negative information, you will probably form failure habits without even thinking about it. A subconscious habit can be formed in a number of ways: taking a wrong turn, making a careless remark, following the lead of someone else's example, thinking as the result of negative attitudes, and so on. But the final result is a habit as powerful as one formed consciously.

Habits, whether good or bad, can be more clearly seen with the aid of this visual image. In your mind, picture a spider as it begins to weave its web. The web starts out as a set of very fragile strands, but as time passes and the spider reinforces it with more threads, it becomes stronger and stronger. Before long, it's strong enough to catch and hold all the food the spider needs.

Habits are formed much the same way. What begins as a fragile thread—a chance act, thought, or attitude—with time and repetition becomes as strong as a steel cable. At that point, you no longer have the habit, the habit has you.

MY ROBOT

I have a little robot
That goes around with me
I tell it what I'm thinking
I tell it what I see.

I tell my little robot
All my hopes and fears.
It listens and remembers
All my joys and tears.

At first my little robot
Followed my command.
But after years of training
It's gotten out of hand.

It doesn't care what's right or wrong,
Or what is false or true.
No matter what I try now,
It tells me what to do.

How are habits broken? The key to breaking undesirable habits is desire. You must first have the desire to break the habit and then follow through with the necessary steps. Please remember, however, that accurately speaking, you don't *break* habits, you *replace* habits. When you quit doing one thing that is habitual, something else will come along to fill the void. To me this fact is very exciting because it means that when you have goals and know what you wish to achieve, you can also develop a plan of action to foster the kind of habits that will bring it about. I have said that success is simple. Isn't this true? Most of us get in ruts in our thinking, our actions, and our living. These have negative influences on our careers, marriages, and relationships with others.

Did you hear about the tombstone that read, "Here lies John Jones. Died at age twenty-one, buried at age seventy-one." Unfortunately, this man was in a rut for fifty years before it became permanent.

The final issue for you is to identify the habits that will insure your success. Several years ago a successful insurance executive named Albert E. N. Gray conducted a study to determine the common denominator of success. It was finally determined that people who are truly successful all share the habit of doing things that failures do not like to do. For example, it is a fact that successful people form the habit of talking to others about things they do not want to talk about—even about things they regard as unpleasant—if discussing them would help them achieve their goals.

Habits are very personal for each of us. In your own case, they must be based on what you personally want out of life. However, there are some general habits common to most successful people. As you look over this list, remember that the principles required for success are a two-edged sword. The same principle that will lead one person to success and happiness will lead another person into the gutter. It is all in how the habit is used—for good or for bad.

Personal Success Habits

Character Habits (These are caught more than taught!)

> *attitude*: Develop an attitude of service and love toward others. You will get back from others what you first give to them.

self-respect: You must respect yourself before you can respect the rights and property of others. Respect must be earned.

good speech: Your words reflect what is inside you. Profanity is often the sign of a weak mind and a poor vocabulary. People who matter can tell a lot about others from the words they use to express themselves.

Work and Study Habits

punctuality: be on time or early for work, appointments, and other engagements.

hard work: Be worth more than you are paid. Hard and valuable work provides the profit from which your salary and raises are paid.

cooperation: If you do not get along with others, the chances are good you will lose your job and never know why.

persistence: When the going gets tough, the tough get going.

study: Education is the foundation for your life.

Financial Habits

save money: Building up a reserve of savings is a must if you are to achieve financial security. Pay yourself first by saving regularly and persistently.

invest money: Look carefully for good opportunities. The money you invest should always yield a return greater than the annual rate of inflation.

Social Habits

responsibility: Be a constructive and contributing member of society.

lawfulness: Obey the laws of the land.

build: Do not destroy. Do your part to guarantee our nation's future and the opportunities of future generations.

charity: Help those that are less fortunate than you in ways that promote their success.

Personal Hygiene Habits

cleanliness: At home and at work, cleanliness will improve your attitude and your self-image, as well as the impression others have of you.

good appearance: Hair, nails, dress, shoes, and so on should always be in top condition. Like it or not, appearance is important for first impressions people will develop of you.

regular checkups: It's important to make sure that you are in the best physical shape possible. Let your doctor help you stay conditioned for success.

In conclusion, good habits are formed by thinking, acting, and repeating the desired activity over and over again. It is difficult in the beginning to turn off the television and get started, but it is worth the effort.

FOOD FOR THOUGHT:

Get in the habit of thinking that
you are a very special and unique person.
You *can* achieve your goals!

CHAPTER 22

Good Communication Skills

How well do you communicate with others? Communication is an area of our lives that causes a great deal of problems. The bottom line of communication is that anything that can be misunderstood, will be misunderstood. Many lives are unfulfilled, jobs are lost, marriages are ruined, and families are divided due to inadequate or poor communication skills.

Communication is a skill that can be developed. All you have to do is understand the process, follow a few simple guidelines, and practice, practice, practice!

As you know, I have tried in this book to relate important ideas to address your needs and ultimately to help you achieve the success you desire. At this point we need to take a careful look at what communication involves and how it can help you move forward in your development.

In the first place, it is important to understand that communication is not merely what you say and how well you say it. It is the total projection of your personality. Everything about you says something to others. Of course, this means that appearance—how you are perceived by others—is a critical component of communication. You may be a fine person on the inside and have good moral values, but if you are not

"Communication is a skill that can be developed. All you have to do is understand the process, follow a few simple guidelines, and practice, practice, practice!"

perceived this way by others, it will be much more difficult for you to communicate with them.

How do others perceive you? I've made a list of words that describe how people are evaluated. Check the ones that you think others would apply to you.

____sharp   ____uncouth
____clean-cut   ____intelligent
____vulgar   ____interesting
____neat   ____charming
____dirty   ____witty
____sloppy   ____dull
____professional   ____happy
____one-track mind   ____carefree

When you leave the privacy of your home and come into contact with people other than your family, you are, in essence, a "walking billboard." Your clothes, personal appearance, mannerisms, behavior, and attitudes all have something to say to others about who you are.

You may have heard the expression, "What you are speaks so loudly that I can't hear a word you are saying." This means your reputation is important in communicating successfully with others. Many people we see about us have great communication skills, but they are avoided because they have bad reputations. Do you know people like this?

In practical terms, this means that impressions count—and first impressions count almost more than you can measure. When you meet a new person, you only have one opportunity to make a good first impression. Should you have further contact with this person, their opinion of you will usually go up or down. If it goes up, you have made a sale; if it goes down, you have lost a sale. If you begin with a good impression, you have already laid the foundation for a productive relationship. As you know, success in life requires that you be able to sell yourself and your ideas to others. Good first impressions developed through careful communication and good appearance will set you on the road to success.

Now that you see the powerful influence communication can have on your success, let's take a closer look at how it actually works. Communication is a process or exchange between two or more people that involves two distinct functions: a communication message must be sent, and then it must be received. From this point forward, I will refer to the individuals involved in the communication process as the sender and the receiver.

Humans, unlike any other creatures on the face of the earth, have the capacity to learn words and their meanings. In any language, the words a person knows and can use successfully form the available vocabulary. When words are linked together, they produce sentences; a series of sentences produces a thought or an idea; a series of thoughts or ideas produces a concept. When a concept is clearly seen in a person's mind, it is visualized in the form of a mental picture. This is where the saying, "Do you get the picture?" comes from.

From this account, we can logically conclude that communication involves transmitting a series of mental pictures or images. The sender sees the mental picture clearly in mind, then chooses words, sentences, thoughts, ideas, and concepts to transfer this mental picture to the minds of the receivers. When the picture is complete and looks the same to both sender and receiver, the communication process is complete.

There is a very important point implicit in this understanding of communication. A person's ability to communicate successfully is tied directly to available vocabulary—the knowledge and ability to use words. If you do not have a good vocabulary, your ability to rebuild mental pictures in the minds of other people will be severely limited.

In addition to the construction of mental pictures in other people's minds, successful communication also involves emotions and feelings. The receiver must feel the same as the sender about the mental picture, if the sender expects the message to have concrete results. Since most people act as a result of feelings or emotions, successful communicators should always take this dimension into consideration when dealing with others. There are important aspects of communication on the receiving end too. We receive information into our minds through one or more of our five senses: sight, hearing, taste, touch, and smell. We see, hear, taste, feel, and smell, and each of these senses is linked directly to our minds. The most important sense for successfully receiving communication is of course hearing (although it is wrong to think that the other senses become inactive).

Many people fail to communicate successfully because they never develop their listening skills. Dr. Carl Stevens, in the article "Is Listening A Lost Art?" argues that we only hear twenty-five to thirty percent of what is said to us. Why? The reason is because approximately ninety percent of our waking time is spent thinking of ourselves. We tend to view the comments of others as interruptions to the flow of our own ideas. If you do not consider yourself a good listener, a great deal of information is available to help you reach your potential. Commit yourself now to research additional sources and develop good listening skills.

The two ways knowledge or information is received and stored in your subconscious mind are repetition and impact with strong emotion or feeling. Repetition is by far the most common of these two modes of learning, and it assumes a proportionally important position in the communication process. According to a recent university study, a message read or heard several times a day for eight days is virtually memorized. At the end of thirty days, the subconscious mind retains ninety percent of the message. On the other hand, a message read or heard only once is sixty-six percent forgotten within 24 hours and is practically washed out of memory in 30 days.

In summary, successful communication is when a person

conveys or transmits a series of mental pictures to a listener or group of listeners. The final goal is to cause a mental and emotional response that motivates other people to action of a specific type. For this goal to be realized the sender must compose the message in a clear and stimulating way, and the receiver must carefully attend to it.

We communicate with others in two basic ways: verbally and nonverbally. When we think about transmitting information to others, *verbal communication* inevitably comes to mind first. This type of information exchange involves sound and most often refers to the spoken word, music, or singing. Verbal communication is formal in approach when we converse by speaking, singing or playing musical instruments to others in a specifically structured performance or speech. This type of communication usually requires some public speaking skills or musical training. Do you have a desire to speak in public? If you do, you should be taking positive steps now to prepare yourself. On the other hand, informal verbal communication encompasses our normal, everyday conversational speech and other verbal means of expression. Non-verbal communication also plays a very important role in our transmission of information. It includes writing, typewriters and other electronic equipment, computers, more strictly non-linguistic forms of expression such as body language and physical gesture.

Have you thought about all the tools that are available to help you improve your communication skills? Words are our most basic communication tools. Without words there would be no thinking, no creativity, no meaningful expression. Even signing, gestures, and body language must be translated into words before they have meaning. The reason most people fail to communicate effectively is because of inadequate or poor vocabulary. A recent study revealed that the average person uses four hundred words or less for eighty percent of everyday conversations. This is true in spite of the fact there are over six hundred thousand words in the English language.

Sound and word processing equipment, typewriters, computers, and other electronic equipment can serve as supplemental tools for your communication needs. These tools can often help you organize your message or present it in a more interesting way. Learn to adapt and use any means you can to help get your message across more effectively.

Your body is also a great communication tool. Develop your skills to use emphasis and expression to reinforce your communication messages. What would Red Skelton, Jack Benny, Carol Burnett, Flip Wilson, Bill Cosby, and Phyllis Diller be without the special expressive skills they have developed? The way you move your body says a lot about your message!

There's an important point I haven't made clear yet. You might be wondering why communication skills are necessary for happiness and success. In any society, a few well-chosen written or spoken words are sufficient for recognizing an educated person. Surveys reveal that a person's knowledge and ability to use language corresponds directly to income, social standing, position, and power. Yes, when you open your mouth and begin to speak, the people who are in a position to help you achieve greater success and have more money and financial security can tell exactly where you are. To say it very simply, your ability to communicate will either help you along or hold you back.

Although the real secret for improving your communication is hard work—practice, practice, practice!— there are a number of concrete suggestions for better communication. Perhaps the most important thing to keep in mind when communicating with others is that whether or not they say so most people want to know "What's in it for me?" To take advantage of this, you could imagine that every person you meet has a large, invisible sign that says, "Make Me Feel Important." Realize that the cardinal sin of communication is to be uninteresting. No one likes to be around a bore, and in this case a bore is someone who talks about himself all the time. The best way you can sell yourself and your ideas is to talk about the other person and develop your listening skills. Look your listener in the eye and really pay attention.

As I have emphasized, you must understand the value of practice. But remember that practice does not make perfect; practice only makes permanent. *Perfect* practice is what produces perfect performance. If you do something wrong, it will not matter how much you practice. You can practice communication skills in a number of specific ways. Keep a dictionary nearby when you are reading to look up words that are unfamiliar to you. Develop a plan to improve your vocabulary; five new words a week or more is a healthy goal. Take a public speaking course if you have the desire to speak in public (I must say, however, that most people in our society today need public speaking skills). Listen to cassette tapes that contain good information and have challenging ideas in their messages.

The keys to successful communication, like success of any kind, are desire, commitment, and practice. Slowly but surely, like the walls of a new building under construction, almost before you know it, you will reach the top.

FOOD FOR THOUGHT:

When you decide to move up the social pyramid you will feel uncomfortable for a time, but the more you try and the longer you stay, the more natural it will feel.

CHAPTER 23

The Life-Long Process of Continuing Education

One evening after the local high school commencement exercises were completed, a graduating senior was heard saying, "Thank God it's over. I'll never open another book as long as I live." The tragedy of this statement is that it is true for millions of people, at least to some degree.

There are approximately sixty million adults in America today who cannot function as responsible members of society. They cannot fill out employment applications or sales contracts or balance checkbooks without the assistance of others. I realize of course that most of these adults did not finish high school, but quit school or dropped out somewhere along the way. My point is only to stress the importance of continuing your education throughout your life. If you are to achieve the success you desire and reach the goals you have established for yourself, education is a project that must never come to an end.

A person in American can earn a great deal of money without the benefit of a good education, but having a good education can do things for you that money cannot buy. It will give you inner satisfaction, contentment, self-esteem, and additional opportunities to move up in society.

"Every good book I read during my lifetime is like an extra one-thousand-dollar deposit in my bank account."

The only requirements for getting a good education are the ability, the desire, and the willingness to read. Reading is the key that will unlock the doors to all kinds of new opportunities. Failure to acquire a desire to read and failure to learn to read properly are the major causes of school dropouts. Students who cannot read effectively get behind, and the farther in school they progress, the farther behind they get. When students reach the point where they give up mentally, they essentially drop out, whether or not they actually leave school.

A lot of people fail to realize that this trend carries over into adulthood as well. Adults drop out of society just like students drop out of school. The person who does not continue to read and grow mentally could be compared to the person who buys a new car and then leaves it locked in the garage for ten years. I am sure you know it is much harder on a car to use it after it has sat neglected for so long than it is to drive it every day. The same principle works where our minds are concerned. What we don't use, we lose.

Your future is bright if you have the desire and incentive to get ahead, while at the same time maintaining balance in your life. It is possible to have all the rewards you seek but it is vital that you keep your eyes on your goals and not dwell on your problems. You should recognize that you have problems—we all do!—but you should not dwell on them or let them get you down. You can never be defeated as long as you are willing to get back up.

Education is one of the best ways available to see beyond present problems to future opportunities. You have to be willing to work at education and reading, however, despite the temptations to waste time that always surround us—like television. It is estimated the average American spends between six and seven hours watching television each day. You might not think that you watch too much television, but I have a question for you. Who is making the money while you are watching television, you or the television producers and sponsors? You can't spend your life in bed or in front of the television and expect to be successful.

For a person to be willing to be successful, there must be a strong motivating desire to implement previous education. You probably know some people who are professional students. In many cases they seek the security of a classroom because they fear what may be out in the real world. Did you hear about the fellow who had a B.A., M.A., and Ph.D. but did not have a J.O.B.? Unless you use your education you have wasted your time.

To be a well-rounded, well-educated person requires a balance of educational activities. In my view, this balance has four basic components. A good basic education will include foundational-level skills in reading, writing, mathematics, and computer use. Beyond this is a good cultural education, which will cultivate appreciation of art, poetry, music, literature, and so forth. Of course, every person must have specialized knowledge relevant to the chosen career, job, or vocation in order to do capable and valuable work. Finally, I think that reading self-help or inspirational books is an excellent way of learning about personal development and human relations.

As you draw close to the end of this book, you may be interested in some books that I would recommend to you for further reading. We all need a break from time to time, and I think there is no better—and more productive—relaxation than a good book. I am sure you will want to read some of these books as part of your long-range plans to keep your mind alert, sharp, alive, growing, and healthy.

Suggested Reading List

General

Books I Love, by John Kieran; *Megatrends*, by John Naisbitt; *The Outline of History*, by H. G. Wells; *The True Believer*, by Eric Hoffer.

Self-Image

Psychocybernetics, by Dr. Maxwell Maltz; *Born to Win*, by Muriel James and Dorothy Jongeward; *The One and Only You*, by Bruce Larson; *The Psychology of Winning*, by Dr. Denis Waitley.

Goal-Setting

See You at the Top, by Zig Ziglar.

Spiritual Life

The Holy Bible; Awake My Heart, by Dr. J. Sidlow Baxter; *Today Is Mine*, by Leroy Brownlow; *Success Motivation and the Scriptures*, by William H. Cook; *Beyond Ourselves*, by Catherine Marshall.

Family Life

Dare to Discipline, by Dr. James Dobson; *The Marriage Builder*, by Lawrence J. Cobb, Jr.; *The Christian Family*, by Larry Christianson.

Health

Aerobics, by Dr. Kenneth Cooper; *How to Stop Worrying and Start Living*, by Dale Carnegie.

Economics

Economics in One Lesson, by Henry Hazlitt; *Believe*, by Richard DeVoss; *Who Owns America?*, by Walter J. Hickel.

Time Management

Managing Your Time, by Ted W. Engstrom and Alex MacKenzie; *How to Get Control of Your Time and Your Life*, by Alan Lakein.

Communication

A good unabridged dictionary; *Thirty Days to Better English*, by Norman Lewis; *The Memory Book*, by Jerry Lucas and Harry Lorayne; *The Quick and Easy Way to Effective Speaking*, by Dale Carnegie; *Effective Public Speaking*, by Dr. Ken McFarland.

Patriotism

One Nation Under God, by Russ Walton; *A Time for Truth*, by William Simon; *The Love of Liberty*, by Leonard E. Read; *Blood and Honor*, by Reinhold Kerstan; *We Hold These Truths*, by Larry McDonald.

Human Relations

How to Win Friends and Influence People, by Dale Carnegie; *The Laws of Success*, by Napoleon Hill; *I Dare You*, by William H. Danforth.

Motivation

The Heart of a Champion, by Bob Richards; *Life Is Tremendous*, by Charles Jones; *The Magic of Believing*, by Claude M. Bristol; *Success through a Positive Mental Attitude*, by W. Clement Stone.

The books listed here are only a handful of the thousands of excellent books covering every conceivable topic available through your local public library or retail book store. I think they will give you a good start, though.

Educational books and tapes are not really an expense, they represent an investment in yourself and your future. When a book is read and applied over an extended period of time, the return it offers to you in hard, cold cash will be many times your original investment.

Where your mind is concerned, it is better to wear out than to rust out. Don't you agree?

FOOD FOR THOUGHT:

Far better it is to dare mighty things, to win glorious triumphs, even though checkered with failure, than to take rank with those poor spirits who neither suffer much nor enjoy much, because they live in the gray twilight that knows not victory or defeat. The one who wins the battle is the one who must first get in the arena.

Theodore Roosevelt

Part Six: Review

I have carefully studied the material covering the question "What Must I Do to Make Success Happen?"

☐ *I know the value of my time in relation to money, and understand what steps I must take to make better use of my productive time.*

☐ *I understand how habits are formed and clearly see the power habits have over my life. I know which of my personal habits will help me succeed and which will cause me to fail.*

☐ *I have to plan to improve my communication skills, and understand that being a good listener is important for my personal success.*

☐ *I understand that learning is a life-long process and not just something I do in school or college. I agree that it is better to wear out than to rust out.*

If you cannot affirm these statements by checking each of the boxes, please go back and reread Part Six before proceeding.

"Hip, hip, hooray! America is great, and we are doing our best to keep it that way!"

America—
The Place for Success

One day a large ship was crossing the Atlantic Ocean. Suddenly a member of the crew rushed up to the captain and said, "Sir, the ship is sinking!" The captain calmly replied, "Let her go; she ain't ours."

It is becoming increasingly evident that more and more people are taking the same attitude about our country, an attitude that in effect says, "I don't care what happens to America, so long as it doesn't affect me personally. If someone is murdered, robbed or raped; if the economy is bad and a lot of people lose their jobs; if interest rates are so high young couples cannot afford to build their own homes; if young people are often hooked on drugs; or if innocent people are killed in automobile accidents by drivers under the influence of alcohol—that's all terrible, but as long as it is happening to someone else, America is still a pretty good place to live." However, people are beginning to realize that the odds are much higher than ever before that the mysterious and distant "someone else" is closer to home than is comfortable. As Pogo said, "We have met the enemy and he is us."

Let me return to my story about the ship for a moment. We must realize, if we live in America and place our hope and faith in America, that we are all on the same ship. If the ship stays afloat, we all have great opportunities; if the ship sinks, we all go down with it, along with the crew and the captain—however naive that captain is.

If you are not completely sold on the good life we have here in America, I want to do my best to sell you on it. You have probably heard the saying, "No man is an island." We are interdependent; we depend on each other for many of life's necessities as well as for some of the finer things. Your opportunity for success and the good life is made possible because of the commitment, work, dedication, and sacrifices of others. We would not be a nation of free men and women were it not for those who fought and died to preserve our way of life.

You can achieve the success you desire because the opportunity is here for you to do it. There's a hitch, however—with opportunity comes responsibility. As a free American citizen, you have a responsibility to protect and preserve opportunities for future generations. As you set out each day to achieve the success you desire, keep this motto in the back of your mind: "The opportunity for me is here because of others, and if the opportunity is to be here for others, it will be because of me."

It is good to be reminded of our heritage, our freedom, our tremendous economic opportunity for material success, but it is vitally important that we teach the American system to our youth. Our human nature decrees that we will only make sacrifices for those things we understand and believe in. Isn't this true?

Because young people in America have no depression to remember and no first-hand experience of war, they can only base their decisions and value judgements about our country on what they read, see, or hear. Many young people view communism as just another major economic system; and to them, it does not really matter which system they live under. What they have not been taught or fail to realize is the ele-

America—The Place for Success 213

ment of military force that is also part of the communist political system. People who live under communist rule have very few personal freedoms. When the people disagree with the official position of the state, military force is used to ensure compliance. If you are a young person reading this book, please answer a question for yourself. If communism is such a great way of life, why would the government of East Germany, for example, need armed guards and a wall to prevent people from getting out? This should give all of us something to think about.

There is also an interesting disparity between promise and fact when it comes to economics. No communist nation produces enough food to feed its own people, but must instead import vast amounts of the food supply. The United States, on the other hand, produces one hundred twenty percent of its needs and exports food to many other countries. Would you rather work and live in a country like the Soviet Union, where five million government agents divide the too little, or like the United States, where five million salespeople market the too much?

President John F. Kennedy said, "The great danger in America is not that the present generation will destroy our system; the great danger is that we will not transmit or teach it to them." Young people must be taught to love, respect, and preserve America.

Are you completely sold yet? I hope so, because America is the greatest place in the world to be. Here are four reasons why America is great:

- The individual citizen has rights and personal freedoms.
- The opportunity for financial and material success is possible because of the competitive free enterprise system.
- The incentive for individual citizens to work hard and

get ahead is preserved because earnings can, for the most part, be kept and personally managed.
- The freedom for individual citizens to live, think, and speak in the manner of their choice is better in America than anywhere else in the world.

Remember: freedom and opportunity must be counterbalanced with responsibility. If you love America as I do, you will be interested to know what you can do personally to keep America free and preserve our opportunities for many years to come. There is quite a bit that you can do. In the first place, the quality and quantity of work you performed in your job or career is linked directly to our nation's economic success. You can help produce fine products of excellent quality at competitive prices to ensure a stable economy.

You can show responsibility for the country by taking part in the governmental process. The government cannot be left solely in the hands of politicians. That is really like leaving the fox to guard the henhouse. If you have strong convictions and want to help preserve our way of life, run for public office. You can also actively take part in government without running for office by exercising your right to vote. Your vote in any election is your voice in the affairs of society. It is also your ticket to a big show called "My Right To Complain." The next time you hear someone complain about how bad the present government is, ask to see their ticket by saying, "Did you vote in the last election?"

If the present trend continues, the next several decades will see more direct citizen involvement in the affairs of government than at any time in our nation's history. As you set out each new day to reach your personal goals, I hope you will consider your citizenship important and will love America enough to run for office or support those political candidates who have America's best interests at heart. Take time to fill out a candidate evaluation form for each candidate you have an opportunity to vote for.

Candidate Evaluation Form

Candidate _____
Position sought _____

Why is this candidate running for office? Remember, actions speak louder than words. List three good reasons this candidate has for seeking public office.

1. _____
2. _____
3. _____

In critical situations involving the public trust or the spending of taxpayers' money, would the candidate vote for or support:
  ☐ special interests?
  ☐ what is best for America?

A vote for America is a vote for your future. You vote for America as a good citizen when you do a number of things. I would guess that you aren't aware of it, but your job performance can be a vote for America. When you perform your job or career in a responsible way and fulfill it to the best of your ability, always looking for ways to improve, you are taking a positive stand for America. When you take a stand and provide an example for truthfulness, righteousness, integrity, and fair play you affirm America. When you are willing to respect the rights and property of your fellow citizens, you show that your vote is for America. And when you become informed about the vital issues facing your community, state, and nation, and either run for office or support political candidates who will keep the sacred trust established by our nation's forefathers, you clearly demonstrate your support for America.

Your success and the success of America is based on the same thing: it is based on the belief in yourself, in your way of life, and in your hope for the future. Belief becomes action and actions produce success. Don't fail to realize that belief is a powerful force. When you believe in the things that matter, you will believe more in yourself and your country. The more you believe, the harder you will work. The harder you work, the more successful you will become. The more successful you become, the more you will know and appreciate the greatness of America.

America is the only ship we have. Let's all work together to keep it afloat!

FOOD FOR THOUGHT:

I Saw Them Tearing a Building Down

I saw them tearing a building down—
A crew of folks in my home town.
With a heave and a ho and a yes, yes yell
They swung a beam and a side wall fell.
I said to the foreman, "Are these people as skilled
As the ones you'd use if you had to build?"
He laughed and said, "Aw, naw, indeed,
Common labor is all I need.
For I can destroy in a day or two
What it took a builder ten years to do."

And I said to myself as I went on my way,
"Which of these roles am I willing to play?
Am I the one who's tearing down
As I carelessly make my way around?
Or am I one who is building with care
So my job, community, state, and country
Will be a little better just because I was there?"

A Personal Note from the Author

As you set out to begin each new day, I hope you will think often of the ideas I have presented in each of these chapters. Reread this book as often as you feel the need. When it comes to your spiritual life, this book was never intended to replace or substitute for the Bible, but I believe it does contain a wealth of practical ideas and problem-solving concepts that will help you live closer to your true potential.

This book has been read and put into action by _____, a very special, unique
your name
person who has a plan and some goals and who is now going to make dreams come true.

Good luck and God bless you!

—Jim Davidson

For Your Information

If you want to obtain additional copies of this revised edition of *How to PLAN YOUR LIFE* they are available from these sources:

- Your local bookstore
- Jim Davidson
  Continuing Education Services, Inc.
  Route 1, Box 49
  Mayflower, AR 72106
  (501) 470-1233
  (Attach a note if you would like the books to be personally autographed.)
- Pelican Publishing Co.
  1101 Monroe Street
  Gretna, LA 70053
  (504) 368-1175

Be sure to listen to the daily radio program, "How to PLAN YOUR LIFE," if it is available in your area. If you would like to have further information about personal appearances by Jim Davidson, at banquets, conventions, conferences, or workshops; How to PLAN YOUR LIFE Seminars for educational, business, or professional groups; How to PLAN YOUR LIFE Education Courses for Public and Private Schools and Colleges; or the "How to PLAN YOUR LIFE" daily radio program, please contact the author at the address or phone number listed above.